Royal Road
to the Isles

Ian McCrorie

Royal Road
to the Isles

---

150 Years of
MacBrayne Shipping

Caledonian MacBrayne
Hebridean and Clyde Ferries

ISBN No. 0-9507166-1-8

Published by Caledonian MacBrayne Limited,
The Ferry Terminal, Gourock PA19 1QP
www.calmac.co.uk

Author: Ian McCrorie

Printed by Fretwells Limited, www.fretwells.co.uk

FOREWORD

by

Dr Harold Mills CB, Chairman of Caledonian MacBrayne Limited
and David MacBrayne Limited

The name David MacBrayne has long been associated with shipping services to the islands and remote communities on the West Coast of Scotland. 2001 marks the 150th anniversary of the forming of the company which came to make his name famous throughout Scotland and beyond.

I am very pleased to have the opportunity to introduce this book by Ian McCrorie marking 150 years of continuous service and tracing the history and achievements of the original company and its successors. These companies developed an extensive network of passenger and cargo services providing what were then, for some communities, the only links with the rest of Scotland. Over the years, the companies and many of their ships and captains have become household names on the West Coast of Scotland, illustrating the mixture of pride, affection and fascination evoked in those who have traversed the routes.

It has been an eventful 150 years. Each generation has seen major changes in social and economic circumstances in the Highlands and Western Islands. The Companies linked with the name of David MacBrayne have been at the heart of these changes, responding to the needs of each decade.

Ian McCrorie's account brings home how innovative and enterprising the Companies have been. They have embraced new technology, with screw vessels replacing paddle steamers, diesel motor vessels replacing steamships, and modern car ferries replacing cargo and passenger ships. Routes have been opened, expanded and withdrawn in response to the needs of passengers and communities. A major early success was the enterprising development of "swift steamers" to convey tourists to all parts of the Highlands, culminating in the introduction in 1878 of what is universally regarded as the most famous and luxurious Scottish paddle steamer of all time - PS *Columba*. When railway connections were established at Strome Ferry, Oban, Kyle of Lochalsh and Mallaig, the services were adapted appropriately. In the last 100 years, the long sea passages from Glasgow to the distant piers of the mainland and the Western Isles have given way to crossings between the mainland and individual islands to accommodate a car-using generation.

A willingness to change in response to changing circumstances and challenges, seeing them as opportunities and not as threats, has been the hallmark of the survival of the Companies sharing the name of David MacBrayne. Today the challenges are

1

as testing as any that past David MacBrayne Companies had to tackle. Today's passengers expect the highest possible level of service in terms of safety, reliability, frequent and convenient timetables, and comfortable ships. The Government naturally seeks good value for the subsidy it provides. The need to comply with the EU Directive on island cabotage demands complex analysis and innovative thinking by those of us currently charged with the well-being of the Company and the communities that it serves. The history of the past 150 years provides a heartening model for us in our endeavours.

Throughout this history of change and development, one constant has been the loyalty of officers and crews through turbulent times and, often, mountainous seas. CalMac, the successor to MacBrayne's, continues to depend on their loyalty and expertise as it introduces state of the art ferries, handles increasingly complex maritime laws and plans for a newly competitive ferry scene. We do indeed live in exciting times!

We hope you will enjoy this volume. CalMac are indebted to Ian McCrorie for his painstaking work to produce a highly readable and profusely illustrated account in celebration of 150 years of remarkable service.

ROYAL ROAD TO THE ISLES

In the beginning

When the Paisley-built iron paddle steamer *Pioneer* cast off from the Broomielaw in Glasgow at six o'clock on the morning of Monday 10 February 1851 nothing appeared to have changed. In fact her owners, Messrs G & J Burns, had just sold her along with other seven steamers, two trackboats and the goodwill of the West Highland trade to their clerk David Hutcheson. To quote the press of the time, it had long been known that the brothers "were anxious to be untramelled from the working details of their smaller steam vessels". Their main preoccupation was in the Irish trade and in connecting services to the Atlantic liners of Cunard, a company in which they also had a considerable interest. George Burns was very much the driving force behind the company and perhaps the immediate catalyst for his action was more personal. On 18 June 1850 one of his Liverpool ships, the *Orion*, had sunk off Portpatrick with great loss of life, among those who perished being his brother and niece; his sister Elizabeth (Beth), who had married one David MacBrayne, died soon afterwards and then on 5 February 1851, only five days before the sale, the boiler of one of his ships, the *Plover*, burst while she was getting up steam in Glasgow: the engineer was killed but his own eldest son had left the engine room just minutes before. The burden of business on him had just become too great. The business itself was none too profitable either, this being around the time of the Highland Clearances when poverty was rife and revenues small.

David Hutcheson was Messrs Burns' chief clerk and had in fact been running the Highland steamers for some time. One of the conditions of sale was that David MacBrayne, the late Beth's son, become one of the partners: and so the firm of David Hutcheson & Co. was born, the three partners being David Hutcheson, his brother Alexander, and David MacBrayne.

The *Pioneer's* route took her to Greenock, Dunoon and Rothesay and on through the Kyles of Bute to Tarbert and Ardrishaig on Loch Fyne. Hers was a daily service, except, of course, on the Sabbath. The previous year she had been owned by a Burns subsidiary, the Castle Steam Packet Company, and had been the 'swift steamer' on the morning and evening runs from Rothesay to Glasgow, while the crack steamer of the fleet, the *Merlin*, took the Ardrishaig run. The *Pioneer* was in fact the only Castle steamer to be transferred to the new firm. Her black funnel with white band was repainted in the new Company colours of scarlet with a narrow black hoop and a black top.

Three other paddle steamers now left Glasgow throughout the year under the Hutcheson flag. The sturdiest, the *Duntroon Castle*, sailed most Thursday mornings

The sturdy paddle steamer *Duntroon Castle* left Glasgow most Thursday mornings in 1851 for Oban, Tobermory and Portree

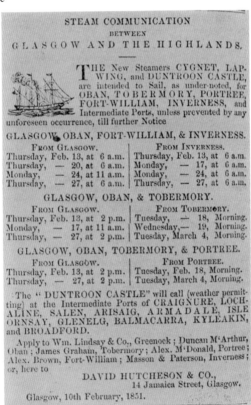

STEAM COMMUNICATION
BETWEEN
GLASGOW AND THE HIGHLANDS.

THE New Steamers CYGNET, LAP-WING, and DUNTROON CASTLE, are intended to Sail, as under-noted, for OBAN, TOBERMORY, PORTREE, FORT-WILLIAM, INVERNESS, and Intermediate Ports, unless prevented by any unforeseen occurrence, till further Notice

GLASGOW, OBAN, FORT-WILLIAM, & INVERNESS.

FROM GLASGOW.	FROM INVERNESS.
Thursday, Feb. 13, at 6 a.m.	Thursday, Feb. 13, at 6 a.m.
Thursday, — 20, at 6 a.m.	Monday, — 17, at 6 a.m.
Monday, — 24, at 11 a.m.	Monday, — 24, at 6 a.m.
Thursday, — 27, at 6 a.m.	Thursday, — 27, at 6 a.m.

GLASGOW, OBAN, & TOBERMORY.

FROM GLASGOW.	FROM TOBERMORY.
Thursday, Feb. 13, at 2 p.m.	Tuesday, — 18, Morning.
Monday, — 17, at 11 a.m.	Wednesday,— 19, Morning.
Thursday, — 27, at 2 p.m.	Tuesday, March 4, Morning.

GLASGOW, OBAN, TOBERMORY, & PORTREE.

FROM GLASGOW.	FROM PORTREE.
Thursday, Feb. 13, at 2 p.m.	Tuesday, Feb. 18, Morning.
Thursday, — 27, at 2 p.m.	Tuesday, March 4, Morning.

The "DUNTROON CASTLE" will call (weather permitting) at the Intermediate Ports of CRAIGNURE, LOCH-ALINE, SALEN, ARISAIG, ARMADALE, ISLE ORNSAY, GLENELG, BALMACARRA, KYLEAKIN, and BROADFORD.

Apply to Wm. Lindsay & Co., Greenock; Duncan M'Arthur, Oban; James Graham, Tobermory; Alex. M'Donald, Portree; Alex. Brown, Fort-William; Masson & Paterson, Inverness; or, here to

DAVID HUTCHESON & CO.,
14 Jamaica Street, Glasgow.

Glasgow, 10th February, 1851.

David Hutcheson & Company's first advertisement in 'The Glasgow Herald'

round the Mull of Kintyre to Oban, Tobermory and Portree, while the other two traversed the Crinan and Caledonian Canals and usually made eventually for Inverness. They were quaint-looking sisters, *Cygnet* and *Lapwing*, which were fitted with rounded bows to assist at the lock-gates, and paddles let in flush with the bulwarks.

While in the Crinan Canal they would come across, at least in summer, the two trackboats *Maid of Perth* and *Sunbeam*, dating from 1847. It was in that year that Queen Victoria and Prince Albert sailed to join the Royal Yacht at Crinan and were transported through the canal on the *Sunbeam*, lavishly fitted out for the purpose. Thus the title "Royal Route" was coined: it was extended to the whole network of services from Glasgow to Inverness and for many years was a major feature of the company's marketing strategy. It is not an exaggeration to say that Her Majesty's visit was probably the single most important factor in opening up the West Highlands.

David Hutcheson's services expanded during the summer season when other 'swift steamers' joined the *Pioneer*. The wooden paddler *Shandon* conveyed passengers off the trackboats at Crinan to Oban and Corpach at the southern end of the Caledonian Canal where they would board the *Edinburgh Castle* for the final leg of the journey to Inverness. Meanwhile the *Dolphin* offered excursions from Oban to the islands of Staffa and Iona and to Glencoe, presumably Ballachulish Pier. On occasion she even sailed to Fort William and on to the head of Loch Eil with a coach connection to Glenfinnan on Loch Shiel. Meanwhile the *Curlew* sailed north from Inverness to Cromarty and Invergordon, although this service was soon to be withdrawn.

Steam navigation had only come to the West Highlands in 1819 when the pioneer paddle steamer *Comet* extended her voyage to Fort William. In the intervening thirty odd years huge progress had been made and new services were started both as a lifeline to the area and for the increasing tourist trade. The routes which Hutcheson inherited were confined to Mull, Skye and the mainland, the latter being especially important as this was the pre-railway era and travel by sea was much more convenient than by stagecoach over indifferent roads. Islay and Lewis were served by other operators while the remaining islands still had to rely on sail.

Early Improvements
The first upgrading was on the Clyde service when in 1852 Hutcheson commissioned from J & G Thomson of Govan the twin-funnelled *Mountaineer*, fitted out lavishly and at fifteen knots on trial arguably the fastest coastal steamer in Europe. Her appearance allowed the *Pioneer* to be transferred to the Corpach-Crinan route and the old *Shandon* to be withdrawn. Even she, however, could not cope with the increasing expectation of the tourists flocking to the Company's premier route and in three years she was transferred to Oban as excursion steamer. New to the Clyde route was the *Iona*, first of the name, which was altogether larger and even faster, thanks to her oscillating rather than steeple engines.

Queen Victoria sailed to join the Royal Yacht at Crinan and was transported through the canal on the trackboat *Sunbeam*. Thus the title "Royal Route" was coined and for many years was a feature of the Company's marketing strategy. A hundred years later, in 1947, the Centenary featured on the front cover of the summer timetable

THE WESTERN ISLES

OF SCOTLAND

1847
CENTENARY
OF THE
ROYAL ROUTE
1947

DAVID MACBRAYNE LIMITED
CLYDE HOUSE, 44 Robertson Street, GLASGOW, C.2

Passengers on the Royal Route would board the *Edinburgh Castle* at the southern end of the Caledonian Canal for the final leg of their journey to Inverness; here the *Edinburgh Castle*, in her later guise as *Glengarry*, is seen entering a lock on the Canal

In 1852 Hutcheson commissioned from J & G Thomson of Govan the twin-funnelled *Mountaineer*; within three years she was transferred from the Clyde to Oban as excursion steamer; the photograph is the famous one of her at Corpach

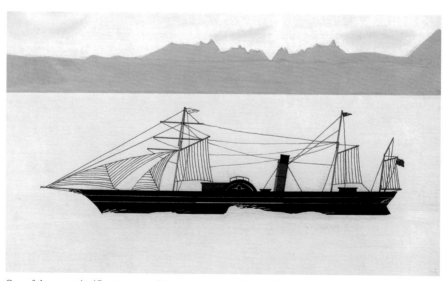

One of the most significant events of the first decade of David Hutcheson & Co was the commissioning in 1853 of the robust paddle steamer *Chevalier* on the weekly voyage from Glasgow to Portree, extended to Stornoway; the painting of the *Chevalier* in the Sound of Sleat commissioned from Alan Neill

One of the most significant events of the new firm's first decade was the commissioning in 1853 of the robust paddle steamer *Chevalier* on a route which for the first time was to extend Hutcheson's sphere of influence to the Outer Isles. She took over from the *Duntroon Castle* on the weekly voyage from Glasgow to Oban, Tobermory and Portree but then ventured across the Minch to Stornoway, the populous capital of the Isle of Lewis. A whole new trade, not just in passengers but also in goods like wool and herring in season, opened up. Unfortunately the *Chevalier* was wrecked within two years and had to be replaced by a new and larger paddler, the first *Clansman*. So heavy was the traffic that at the same time the service was doubled, the second steamer being originally the redundant Oban excursion vessel *Dolphin* and from 1858 the second hand *Stork*, formerly one of the Messrs Burns' Irish steamers.

It was in 1855 that a crucial event occurred when David Hutcheson & Company was awarded its first mail contract, which allowed it later to use the description "Glasgow & Highland Royal Mail Steamers". The Postmaster General was to provide much needed funds for many years to come.

The other expansion of the fifties took place on the Clyde. On 12 February 1857 the Company took over the assets and goodwill of the Glasgow & Lochfyne Steam Packet Company: one of the assets was the *Mary Jane*, which had been built for the Glasgow-Stornoway trade in 1846 and which was destined to be a prominent member of the fleet for many years. The other vessel acquired was the *Inverary Castle* (sic), already almost twenty years old. The two ships, kenspeckle in their red, white and black funnels, sailed on alternate days between Glasgow and Inverary, only making a leisurely single journey each day. Six weeks later Hutcheson also took over the Glasgow and Highland Steam Packet Company and so the *Maid of Lorn* entered the fleet. She was soon sold but had to be bought back when the *Lapwing* sank following a collision off the Mull of Kintyre: she was re-named *Plover* and sailed for many years along with the *Cygnet* on the Glasgow-Inverness route.

New Ships for Old
From the marine point of view, the next two advances came in 1861 when Hutcheson ordered his first screw steamer, the *Fingal*, for the Stornoway route in succession to the *Stork*. Previously paddle steamers had graced every route. This was, however, the time of the American Civil War and the Confederates of the south set out to obtain fast manoeuvrable vessels capable of "running the Yankees' blockade". They looked to the Clyde and Western Isles of Scotland. After only four months' service the *Fingal* was on her way across the Atlantic and David Hutcheson was very much richer as a result: for the first time he had real money behind him. The *Dolphin* followed as, in 1862, did the flagship of the fleet, the *Iona*, but the latter only reached Gourock Bay before being sunk following a disastrous collision, fortunately without loss of life. A new *Iona* was built for the 1863 season but Hutcheson succumbed to the profit motive once more and sold her to the Confederates, known in the press as the 'Emperor of China', a somewhat spurious method of keeping their activities secret. She fared little better than her predecessor, being sunk near Lambay Island, near Dublin.

In 1857 David Hutcheson took over the assets and goodwill of the Glasgow & Lochfyne SP Co, and with it the *Inverary Castle* of 1839, seen here approaching the pier at Kames in the Kyles of Bute

David Hutcheson bought the *Mary Jane* in 1857; she was destined to be a prominent member of the fleet for many years to come. She is seen here at Tarbert in her rôle as Loch Fyne cargo steamer

The second improvement of 1861 was the building of the paddle steamer *Fairy* - she was the first member of the fleet to have a deck saloon to provide shelter for her passengers, her owner now having the wherewithal for such extravagances. Previously the ships were largely 'flush-decked' and shelter, dining facilities and, where appropriate, rudimentary sleeping accommodation had all been provided below water level. She was built for the service on the Caledonian Canal as a partner for the *Edinburgh Castle*, but, in a rare case of misjudgment, Hutcheson had overestimated the potential of the route and after a year she was transferred to Oban as a consort to the *Mountaineer*. This allowed an extension of the Oban excursion programme to include a two day trip to Loch Coruisk and Portree in Skye and even on to Gairloch in Wester Ross. By the autumn of 1863, however, after a short spell replacing the *Iona*, she too was sold foreign.

The upshot of all this activity was that two vessels needed urgent replacement, one for the Stornoway route and one for the prestige Glagow-Ardrishaig service. The screw steamer *Clydesdale* (1862) and the magnificent two-funnelled *Iona* of 1864 respectively gave many years' outstanding service to the Company. The latter was very much the 'society boat' among Clyde steamers, transporting the gentry and others to their sporting estates in the north. She inherited the deck saloons of her short-lived predecessor and in general was furnished sumptuously both inside and out, the gilded scrollwork on her bow, stern and paddle boxes matching her accommodation "in the most magnificent style of art, combining indeed the beauty, comfort and all the facilities of a perfectly furnished private mansion".

In just over a dozen years David Hutcheson & Co had brought a virtual revolution to sea transport in the West Highlands and Islands. Only three paddle steamers of the eight the firm had inherited were still in service - and they were to last for several more years - and the speed, tonnage and luxurious accommodation of the ships built or acquired could not have been imagined in 1851.

Three Memorable Steamers
It was in 1866 that David Hutcheson - and the ever more influential David MacBrayne - gave a real boost to the profile of the Royal Route by building three memorable vessels to enhance the fleet. First came the *Gondolier*, a saloon paddler specially designed for working the locks in the Caledonian Canal. A real effort was being made to increase traffic on the connecting service between Banavie and Inverness and this time the venture was successful, as the *Gondolier* and *Edinburgh Castle* maintained a partnership on the Canal and Loch Ness for many years to come.

The twin-funnelled *Chevalier* was the next, built for the middle leg of the route between Crinan and Corpach. Lying overnight at Corpach, at the head of Loch Linnhe and the foot of the Caledonian Canal, she left early in the morning with passengers brought from Inverness the previous day and sailed south to Oban and Crinan. There the travellers would disembark for a leisurely trip through the Crinan Canal to Ardrishaig, where the *Iona* would be waiting for the journey onwards to Glasgow. In the afternoon the *Chevalier's* route was reversed.

Hutcheson renamed the *Maid of Lorn* and as *Plover* she sailed for many years on the Glasgow-Inverness route

The *Iona* was placed on the prestige Glasgow-Ardrishaig service in 1864 and gave many years' outstanding service to the Company; she is seen here in early condition at Ardrishaig

The first of three memorable vessels built in 1866 was the *Gondolier*, a saloon paddler specially designed for working the locks in the Caledonian Canal; passengers are seen embarking at Fort Augustus

The twin-funnelled *Chevalier* was built for the middle leg of the Royal Route between Crinan and Corpach; here she is seen as built with very tall thin funnels

The third vessel built for David Hutcheson & Co in 1866 was the quaint twin-screw steamer *Linnet* for service in the Crinan Canal; she is seen here at Crinan in 1901

P.S. *Clansman* ran aground in 1869; the following year she was replaced in grand style with a new vessel of the same name, but she was a screw ship rather than a paddler; she is seen here at Stornoway

It was for the Crinan Canal itself that the third 1866 vessel was built - the quaint twin-screw steamer *Linnet*, just 86 feet in length and resembling a floating tram rather than a conventional ship. With her commissioning the days of the trackboats drawn by horses along the bank were over, although the *Sunbeam* was retained for a few years to deal with the occasional overspill. Anyone making the journey from Glasgow to Inverness in the summer season would now board four new crack ships, the *Iona*, *Linnet*, *Chevalier* and *Gondolier* for a journey where comfort and luxury were of the very essence. The Oban excursions could once again be expanded and the trip to Skye which had lapsed after the withdrawal of the *Fairy* was revived by the *Pioneer*, displaced from the Corpach-Crinan station.

All-the-Way Sailings
There was little growth in the all-the-way passenger and cargo sailings in the sixties, except that in 1863 a single screw steamer *Staffa* was added to the fleet. Of the three smallish vessels, *Cygnet*, *Plover* and *Staffa*, two could now sail all the way to and from Inverness while the third, usually the *Plover*, concentrated on transporting goods to and from the remote communities in the Sound of Mull and surrounding area, including Loch Sunart and Ballachulish. With road transport in the isolated areas so primitive goods were consigned by ship and landed at remote piers or in many cases by rowing boat. The decade ended with misfortune when in July 1869 the *Clansman* ran aground in thick fog off the Mull of Kintyre.

The 1870s were no less expansive as far as the Hutcheson empire was concerned. The *Clansman* had urgently to be replaced: this was done in grand style with a new vessel of the same name, but she was a screw ship rather than a paddler. She gave yeoman service over several years and, despite her arduous and unromantic employment, she was still fitted out to the normal high standards of the fleet with ornamental carving on her clipper bow and stern.

Rejuvenation
In 1875, nine years after the *annus mirabilis* when three new vessels were added to the fleet, three of the oldest steamers dating from the forties were thoroughly renovated and upgraded to be given a completely new lease of life. First came the *Pioneer* which was lengthened, given a second funnel and provided with the now obligatory deck saloons so that she could be more worthy of her calling as a full-blown Oban excursion steamer. The *Edinburgh Castle* was also taken in hand. She and the *Gondolier* had been working the Caledonian Canal route each making the single journey each day - but they were not a good match. She too was therefore lengthened, had her stem altered, had short deck saloons fitted fore and aft and had her funnel moved to the more 'modern' position farther forward. She even had her name changed - to *Glengarry* - and as such became a more equal partner on the Canal.

When the Inveraray cargo steamer *Mary Jane* was upgraded similarly she not only was physically enhanced but was also permitted into the ranks of 'swift steamer' with a new name - *Glencoe*. She too was lengthened - at 165 feet she was now almost midway between the *Iona* at 255 feet and the *Cygnet* at 77 feet. She lost her

In 1875 the *Pioneer* was lengthened and given a second funnel and a deck saloon so that she could be more worthy of her calling as a full-blown Oban excursion steamer; she is seen here at Corpach in this condition

The Inveraray cargo steamer *Mary Jane* was upgraded in 1875 and renamed *Glencoe*; she is seen here in the 1890s in a later phase of her career at Port Ellen

mainmast but gained a substantial deck saloon aft. Transferred to Oban as an excursion steamer she took over the Skye and Gairloch route. This allowed the *Mountaineer* to operate daily to and from Fort William and the rejuvenated *Pioneer* was able to take up the 'premier' trip to Staffa and Iona. The *Mary Jane* was not replaced on the Clyde and it is interesting that a few years later the Loch Fyne merchants were so dissatisfied at having only one steamer that they built a new screw ship of their own to run on the alternate days. The single remaining Hutcheson vessel *Inveraray Castle*, incidentally spelt the modern way from 1874, had herself twice been lengthened but not otherwise improved.

The official Royal Route took the Victorian traveller through the Crinan Canal and then on by the *Chevalier* to Oban, but there was an alternative. Passengers disembarking from the *Iona* at Ardrishaig could be taken by coach to Ford, at the south end of the inland loch, Loch Awe, there to board a small wooden screw steamer *Queen of the Lake* for the sail up the considerable length of the waterway. They would disembark at the north end where the formidable Pass of Brander swept up from the loch and would complete their journey by coach. The little steamer was sold to David Hutcheson & Co in 1875. A year later she was replaced by a larger iron steamer, appropriately named *Lochawe*, built on the Clyde and transported in sections to Ford. The Company had neatly consolidated their position on the alternative and equally scenic route to Oban.

The Islay Trade
The other event of the mid-seventies was of greater significance. The southern island of Islay had been served by steam since 1825 but the Hutcheson influence had never extended there. Instead a series of vessels plied to the island, culminating in the *Islay*, a handsome vessel sporting two black funnels, two masts and a clipper bow. Her owners eventually decided to sell out to the superior might of David Hutcheson & Co and in February 1876 the *Islay* was taken over, along with the goodwill of the Islay trade. She left Glasgow twice a week for the island and crossed once to West Loch Tarbert, the nearest suitable pier on the mainland, where connection could be made with the *Iona* for Glasgow. This was a time of great prosperity and expansion for the numerous whisky distilleries in Islay: the significance of this was not lost on the Company.

Hutcheson's Legacy
David Hutcheson was now 77, a fair age in Victorian terms and, in 1876, he decided to retire, his younger brother following two years later. The way he developed the Royal Route with his 'swift steamers', expanded the excursion trade, especially out of Oban, with ever more sumptuous vessels, increased his influence in the general trade between Glasgow and the Highlands and Islands and took over the assets of several competitors, is legendary. Sadly he only had two years to enjoy his retirement. David Hutcheson was thought so highly of by the people whose transport needs he served that he is commemorated by a monument on the Island of Kerrera seen to this day by the passengers on the ferries as they leave Oban Bay. The inscription reads:
"Erected by a grateful public in memory of David Hutcheson, by whose energy and

In 1876 an iron steamer was built on the Clyde and transported in sections to Ford on Loch Awe for service on the loch as an alternative to the Royal Route to Oban via Crinan; the *Lochawe* is seen here at Ford Pier

David Hutcheson is commemorated by a monument on the Island of Kerrera seen to this day by the passengers on the ferries as they leave Oban Bay.

John Ramsay

17

enterprise the benefits of greatly improved steam communication were conferred on the West Highlands and Islands of Scotland".

Columba - Second to None

David MacBrayne was already very much the driving force in the Company, but in 1877 he himself faced for the first time a genuine competitor on his Clyde route. A crack paddle steamer *Lord of the Isles* had been placed on a new tourist route sailing daily between Glasgow and Inveraray and in fittings and in speed she fairly easily eclipsed the *Iona*. Always one to take up a challenge, MacBrayne decided to ask J & G Thomson to build a ship which would outshine her rival. The shipbuilders, having just moved from Govan to a new yard at Clydebank, responded magnificently and in the *Columba* produced arguably the greatest Clyde steamer of all time. She was the first of the Company's vessels to be built of steel, at the time in the experimental stage of development; she was until the 1990s the only Clyde steamer over 300 feet; she had deck saloons the full width of the hull (previously they were narrow with alleyways round them); she had accommodation and fittings second to none and she even sported the United Kingdom's first floating Post Office - and a barber's shop. At both Tarbert and Ardrishaig extensive pierworks were required to accommodate her but once in service the *Columba* exceeded her owners' expectations and ensured that the prestige of the Royal Route was upheld. Meanwhile the *Iona* in 1878 was relegated to a secondary service half an hour later sailing via the two railheads at Greenock, Steamboat Quay and Prince's Pier, to the railway terminus at Wemyss Bay and then on direct to Ardrishaig. In 1879 she merely offered cruises to a new pier at Skipness in Kintyre during Glasgow Fair, although she was also used at the beginning and end of the season on the main roster when traffic was lighter. The 'swift steamer' route, as distinct from the Loch Fyne cargo run, had originally been seasonal but had gradually expanded until it was offered for some ten months of the year, the smaller and more economical *Mountaineer* being the usual winter boat. From the winter of 1867/68 it had become daily, although from November 1869 the winter roster started and finished at Greenock and not Glasgow.

Mail Services

In 1877 another attempt was made to expand the Company's operations to Inverness and a screw steamer *Lochiel* was commissioned for this purpose. She lasted only a few winter months in the trade before she was replaced by the smaller *Fingal*. Unlike the *Lochiel* she concentrated purely on serving the small communities on either side of Loch Ness, giving a daily run between Inverness and Fort Augustus. Thus the Loch Ness Mail run was born. Meanwhile, having consolidated his position on Islay, MacBrayne had realised the potential of having a daily steamer crossing from the island to West Loch Tarbert connecting into the great *Columba*. The *Glencoe* inaugurated the run in November 1878 but in the following season the *Lochiel*, being spare, was transferred to the station. The venture was immediately successful. It was the Company's first island to mainland Royal Mail service in the Western Isles, the Island of Bute on the Clyde having already been served by the Ardrishaig mail steamer. The *Lochiel*, incidentally, had spent the suumer of 1878 on a new venture - a trip up Loch Etive above the treacherous Falls of Lora from Connel

THE **ROYAL** ROUTE

GLASGOW AND HIGHLAND ROYAL MAIL STEAMERS.

David MacBrayne.

R.M.S Columba

In 1878 J & G Thomson produced in the *Columba* arguably the greatest Clyde steamer of all time; she became the subject of David MacBrayne's official postcard advertising the 'Royal Route' and his 'Glasgow and Highland Royal Mail Steamers'

The great *Columba* is seen at Ardrishaig in her first season, 1878

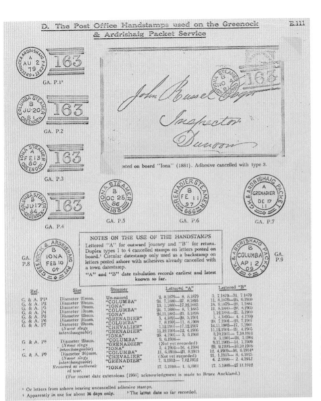

GA. P.1ª

GA. P.2

GA. P.3

...nted on board "Iona" (1881). Adhesive cancelled with type 3.

GA. P.4

GA. P.5

GA. P.6

GA. P.7

GA. P.8

GA. P.9

NOTES ON THE USE OF THE HANDSTAMPS

Lettered "A" for outward journey and "B" for return. Duplex types 1 to 4 cancelled stamps on letters posted on board.¹ Circular datestamp only used as a backstamp on letters posted ashore with adhesives already cancelled with a town datestamp.

"A" and "B" date tabulation records earliest and latest known so far.

Ref.	Size	Steamer	Lettered "A"	Lettered "B"
G. & A. P1ª	Diameter 22mm.	Un-named	2, 8.1879—8, 8.1879	3, 7.1879—31, 7.1879
G. & A. P2	Diameter 20mm.	"COLUMBA"	24, 7.1880—27, 8.1895	11, 8.1879—26, 6.1900
G. & A. P3	Diameter 20mm.	"IONA"	18, 7.1880—17.12.1883	16, 9.1879—29, 7.1884
G. & A. P4	Diameter 20mm.	"COLUMBA"	20, 7.1880—8, 7.1895	11, 8.1881—29, 8.1900
G. & A. P5	Diameter 19mm.	"IONA"	26.11.1885—23, 5.1898	1.12.1884—25, 5.1900
G. & A. P6	Diameter 19mm.	"GRENADIER"	5, 4.1897—30, 5.1901	5, 4.1885—4, 4.1910
G. & A. P7	Diameter 22mm.	"COLUMBA"	7, 8.1901—11, 8.1908	20, 7.1901—23, 7.1907
	(some slugs interchangeable)	"CHEVALIER"	1.12.1901—17.12.1907	14.11.1905—17, 5.1907
G. & A. P8	Diameter 25mm.	"GRENADIER"	11.10.1900—12, 4.1906	11.12.1901—31, 4.1905
	(Some slugs interchangeable)	"IONA"	29, 4.1901—3, 5.1906	3.10.1901—7.10.1911
		"COLUMBA"	9, 6.1904—	9, 5.1901—24, 5.1904
"	Diameter 25mm.	"GRENADIER"	(Not yet recorded)	9.11.1903—14, 7.1909
G. & A. P9	(Name slugs interchangeable)	"IONA"	3, 4.1901—16, 4.1904	29, 9.1903—10.10.1908
		"COLUMBA"	11, 6.1910—23, 8.1913	12, 4.1906—16, 4.1913
	Renamed as outbreak of war.	"CHEVALIER"	(Not yet recorded)	21, 1.1915—8, 4.1915
		"IONA"	7, 5.1912—7.12.1912	4, 2.1910—2, 4.1912
		"IONA"	17, 5.1910—1, 6.1911	17, 5.1908—27.11.1912

(For recent date extensions (1966) acknowledgment is made to Bruce Auckland.)

¹ Or letters from ashore bearing uncancelled adhesive stamps.
² Apparently in use for about 36 days only.   ³ The latest date so far recorded.

A page from a collector's album showing the various postal cancellations used on the Royal Mail steamers like the *Columba*

GLASGOW TO ISLAY, (via Tarbert).

	GLASGOW TO ISLAY.	A.M.	ISLAY TO GLASGOW.	A.M.
"COLUMBA" OR "IONA."	FROM Glasgow (Daily April till October) at	7 0	FROM Port-Ellen (Daily except Tuesday) at	8 30
	Greenock (Daily during the Year) ,,	9 0	Port-Askaig (Every Tuesday) ,,	8 30
	Prince's Pier ,,	9 3		
	Kirn ,,	9 25	Gigha (South end.Daily except Tuesday,North end, Every Tuesday)	10 5
	Dunoon ,,	9 35		
	Innellan ,,	9 50	Clachan Ferry ⎱	10 40
	Rothesay ,,	10 15	Ardpatrick Ferry ⎰	
	Colintraive ,,	10 40	Dunmore Ferry ,,	10 55
	Tighnabruaich ,,	10 55	Tarbert (west) ,,	11 25
	Tarbert (east) ,,	11 45		
COACH	⎧ Tarbert (east) ,, about	11 50	⎧ Tarbert (west) daily about	11 30
	⎩ Tarbert (west),, ,,	12 35P	⎩ Tarbert (east) ,, ,,	12 5P
"SWIFT STEAMER."	Tarbert (west) ,,	12 40	Tarbert (east) ,,	1 40
	Dunmore Ferry ,,	1 10	Tighabruaich ,,	2 45
	Ardpatrick Ferry ⎱	1 25	Colintraive ,,	3 0
	Clachan Ferry ⎰		Rothesay ,,	3 30
	Gigha (South end, Daily except Monday, North end, Every Monday)	2 0	Innellan ,,	3 55
			Dunoon ,,	4 15
	ARRIVING AT		Kirn ,,	4 25
	Port-Ellen (Daily except Monday) about	3 40	Prince's Pier ,,	5 0
			Greenock ,,	5 5
	Port-Askaig (Every Monday) ,,	3 30	ARRIVING AT Glasgow ,,	6 45

The *Lochiel* became the Islay mail steamer in 1879; her timetable is extracted from "Summer Tours - Glasgow to the Highlands" of 1880

Ferry to the head of the loch. This was a miscalculation as the trade never developed and the experiment was never repeated - hence the availablility of the ship for Islay.

In June 1879, MacBrayne, now the sole partner of David Hutcheson & Co, decided to carry on the business of the company in his own name, simply as David MacBrayne. He himself was already 65 years of age. One feature of his influence was the production of the annual gilt-edged hardback "Summer Tours in Scotland", now very much collectors' items, containing detailed descriptions of each of the tourist routes and circular tours offered by his ships. It is alleged that he wrote much of the material himself.

Railway Connections
It was in the 1880s that railways first impinged on the MacBrayne story within the West Highlands. The Dingwall & Skye Railway, a subsidiary of the Highland Railway, had first won through to the west coast in 1870 - at Strome Ferry in Loch Carron. Connections were made by steamer to Portree and Stornoway but the D & S operated them themselves. It was an unsuccessful venture, thanks largely to poor judgment on the part of the directors, and Hutcheson/MacBrayne had been approached on several occasions to take over. David Hutcheson had resisted the overtures but David MacBrayne saw the railways not as a threat but as an opportunity. At last in April 1880 he came to an agreement and inaugurated his new mail run from Portree with the *Lochiel*, the *Glencoe* taking over during the summer season when the screw steamer was back at Islay. Connection was made at Portree with the *Clansman or Clydesdale* for Stornoway. He could spare the *Glencoe* for his new route as momentous events were happening at Oban and she had been declared redundant there. In a sense the *Glencoe* merely substituted Strome Ferry for Oban as her mainland terminal as she had already been running to Skye.

The Callander & Oban Railway, sanctioned since 1865, reached Oban in time for a grand opening on 30 June 1880, the railhead being at the south of Oban Bay at a new wharf appropriately called the Railway Pier. MacBrayne, rather apprehensive about the competition the new form of transport would have on his Royal Route of steamers, brought the *Iona* round from the Clyde and she actually carried the VIPs on a cruise round Kerrera and Lismore on this auspicious occasion. The *Iona* had been all but redundant since the commissioning of the *Columba*, and was therefore available to take over the daily excursion from Oban to Staffa and Iona, the *Pioneer* replacing the *Glencoe* on the Skye and Gairloch run. In the event the railway generated extra traffic and Oban entered a boom period. The *Iona's* appearance was very timely. The following year she and the *Chevalier* exchanged places and the *Iona* became the Corpach-Crinan steamer.

MacBrayne Expansion
It was in the summer of 1881 that MacBrayne's next Royal Mail service was inaugurated when the little *Cygnet* commenced sailing daily from Tobermory and the Sound of Mull piers and ferries to Oban in connection with the new trains. At the same time the direct sailing from Glasgow ceased and the *Plover* transferred to the Inverness route in lieu of the *Cygnet*. The *Pioneer* in fact took over the Mull run

A portrait of David MacBrayne (1814-1907) who in June 1879 decided to carry on the business of the company in his own name

One feature of David MacBrayne's influence was the production of an annual gilt-edged hardback "Summer Tours in Scotland"; the illustration shows the *Grenadier* and *Iona* in Oban Bay from the 1891 book

The Callander & Oban Railway reached Oban in time for a grand opening on 30 June 1880

The *Cavalier*, notable for being the first vessel in the fleet with electric light installed, replaced the *Plover* on the Glasgow-Inverness run in 1883; she is seen here in a lock in the Caledonian Canal

later that year and remained on it. The *Cygnet* became spare for a short time before she was wrecked near Lochailort in 1882. The *Plover* too was withdrawn early in 1883, being replaced by a handsome new screw steamer *Cavalier*, notable for being the first vessel in the fleet with electric light installed, another incidental improvement made by David MacBrayne.

In November 1881 came yet another mail service for David MacBrayne when he took over the run from Stornoway to Ullapool previously operated by an old-fashioned paddle steamer *Ondine*. It was the *Lochiel* which once again took up the sailing but this time there was no vessel to take her place at Islay. MacBrayne had to resort to expensive chartering to keep that service going in the height of the season when all the fleet was occupied. Normally charters only took place in winter to help with the annual overhaul programme. By 1885 it was obvious that there were many advantages to be gained by switching the mainland terminal for the Stornoway mail run from Ullapool to Strome Ferry with its ready connection into the Highland Railway. Despite strong objections from the folk of Ullapool who claimed that their township was being set back several years, the change was made. It was to be almost a century before the route returned to Ullapool.

Just as notable, however, as the new mail route to Stornoway was the commissioning for the Glasgow-Stornoway trade of the *Claymore*, launched in July 1881 but not entering service until January of the following year - the first ship built for David MacBrayne himself. She was to the all-the-year-round all-the-way passenger and cargo screw ships what the *Columba* was to the swift paddle steamers. She has been variously described as a 'noble craft', a 'real beauty' and 'lovely to look upon'. Leaving Glasgow every Thursday around one o'clock she made for Greenock and then on to Oban and various north mainland ports before crossing the Minch to Stornoway, spending the Sabbath there (except on the occasions when she continued to Scrabster Roads, Thurso with herring fishers) and returning on Monday afternoon. In this she supplanted the *Clansman*, which took over the secondary Monday sailing. By cascading his ships, the redundant *Clydesdale* moved to the biweekly Glasgow-Islay service allowing the *Islay* to move to Oban for the Skye run and the *Pioneer* to be spared for the new Mull mail service. This arrangement actually only lasted one year as in 1883 the *Islay* returned to her usual haunts, the *Clydesdale* moved to Strome Ferry and the *Glencoe* operated once again from Oban to Skye.

The new business had achieved miracles in only four years but David MacBrayne had no desire to stand still. The Oban excursion service needed upgrading - three vessels, though thoroughly renovated, were between thirty and forty years old - and a vessel had to be found for Islay in summer, the Lochness steamer *Fingal* carrying out the service in winter. In 1885 he went to J & G Thomson for the last time and they produced a very pretty two-funnelled paddle steamer complete with clipper bow and bowsprit, though with very old-fashioned oscillating engines. The *Grenadier* was placed on the Oban-Skye-Gairloch route. The *Glencoe* returned to Strome Ferry and the *Clydesdale* became spare. The other acquisition of the year was at the opposite end of the marine spectrum. The *Lough Foyle* was working out of Glasgow for the notorious Sabbath breaker Henry Sharp until an Act of

The *Claymore* of 1881 has been variously described as a 'noble craft', a 'real beauty' and 'lovely to look upon'. She is seen here dwarfing her consort on the Glasgow-Stornoway run, the *Clansman*, at Tobermory

The very pretty two-funnelled paddler *Grenadier*, complete with clipper bow and bowsprit, was commissioned in 1885; the following year she took up the Staffa and Iona excursion from Oban; she is seen here lying off Staffa

25

Parliament put a stop to selling drink on Sunday sailings, the only reason for their taking place in the first place. MacBrayne 'rescued' her. Having altered her extensively to bring her up to his traditional high standard, the *Lochness*, as she was renamed, commenced a very respectable if humdrum career as the Loch Ness mail steamer. This allowed the *Fingal* to be employed between West Loch Tarbert and Islay all year round.

The next problem David MacBrayne had to solve once again originated on the Clyde. A rival business, owned by a well-known Clyde master Alexander Williamson, had the temerity to invade his territory and place a steamer on a weekend service to Tarbert and Ardrishaig, berthing over the Sabbath at the latter port. In retaliation, MacBrayne returned the *Iona* to the Clyde and for almost twenty years she would leave Ardrishaig every morning at a quarter to six for the Broomielaw, Glasgow, returning at half past one. The opposition melted, but the price was that the *Chevalier* had to return to the Corpach-Crinan route, the *Grenadier* had to take over at Staffa and Iona, where she remained for many years, and Oban-Skye-Gairloch was once again in the hands of the veteran *Glencoe*, the *Clydesdale* once again gaining full employment at Strome Ferry.

It is perhaps not surprising, then, that MacBrayne tried again to provide his popular Oban-Skye route with a new vessel. In 1888 he went to McArthur of Paisley for the *Fusilier*, almost a scaled down *Grenadier* with a single funnel. A useful and economical ship, she was duly placed on the Skye and Gairloch route. Once again an exercise in musical chairs resulted, the *Glencoe* going back yet again to Strome Ferry and the *Clydesdale* trying out a new service, largely for fishermen, from Glasgow to Thurso. It is of interest that in 1887 MacBrayne had bought over from the owner of the Gairloch Hotel his small screw steamer *Maree* which ran on the specially beautiful Loch Maree. Connections were made with the Gairloch steamer and the Highland Railway.

The Outer Isles in the Picture
Meanwhile momentous events were taking place in the other sector of the business. MacBrayne had been upgrading some of his passenger and cargo vessels - in 1885, for example, he placed a second-hand screw steamer *Ethel* on the Inverness run in lieu of the old *Staffa* - and in 1887 he bought over the *Aros Castle* which belonged to one of his competitors, Martin Orme. This vessel had been designed for service through the Crinan Canal and so was only 84 feet in length and had a speed of a mere 8 knots. MacBrayne renamed her *Handa* and placed her on his first ever Outer Isles mail service from January 1888. She was timetabled to leave Portree three times a week and negotiate the Sea of the Hebrides as she headed for Tarbert, Harris and then sailed back to Skye, but to Dunvegan on the west coast. The *Claymore* and *Clansman* called at Tarbert on occasions en route to Stornoway but the *Handa* was the first regular visitor. It did not take MacBrayne long to realise that the little *Handa*, sturdy as she was, was woefully inadequate for his new service. In February he bought the *Adela* which was lying idle in Ayr Harbour, renamed her *Staffa* and by March commissioned her on his new route. At the same time, following bitter complaints that their mail was still being delivered by sail, the people of Lochmaddy

MacBrayne 'rescued' the *Loch Foyle* from her life as a Sunday Breaker, brought her up to his traditional high standard and as *Lochness* she commenced a very respectable if humdrum career as the Loch Ness mail steamer; she is seen here at Fort Augustus in 1887

A useful and economical ship, the *Fusilier* was placed on the route from Oban to Skye and Gairloch; she is seen here approaching Oban

A deck view of the *Fusilier*

In 1887 MacBrayne bought over the *Aros Castle* from Martin Orme, renamed her *Handa* and placed her on his first ever Outer Isles mail service from January 1888; she is seen here leaving Oban

in North Uist had their township added to the roster. Connection, incidentally, could be made with the mainland through the Strome Ferry mailboat at Portree.

The last major expansion of the MacBrayne empire came a year later, in April 1889. The Highland Fisheries Company of Oban had three years previously broken completely new ground when they won the mail contract to provide a service three days a week from Oban to the islands of Coll, Tiree, Barra and South Uist. These islands had been served previously only by ships of Martin Orme and John McCallum sailing weekly from Glasgow. They now had regular steamer calls for the first time. When Highland Fisheries withdrew David MacBrayne immediately stepped in to provide the service - with the *Clydesdale* leaving Oban every Monday, Wednesday and Friday at six o'clock in the morning and returning on the other days via the west coast of Skye. (She was lying spare as her Thurso venture had proved a non-starter.)

The eighties, then, were the first decade of David MacBrayne ownership in his own right and what he achieved was truly phenomenal. He built four new ships, including the admirable *Claymore* and *Grenadier*, and purchased a total of fourteen others. Some of these were large coastal ships which traded, largely under charter, to various European ports while others were small 'tramps' carrying coal, limestone and pavement round the British coast. The expansion in routes, however, was even more significant. Apart from consolidating his new route to Islay from West Loch Tarbert, he acquired mail contracts for Loch Ness and Mull, for Portree and Stornoway from Strome Ferry, for Tarbert, Harris and Lochmaddy from Portree and for Lochboisdale in South Uist, Castlebay in Barra, Tiree and Coll from Oban.

As in the sixties, however, the 1880s ended in misfortune. In 1889 the old *Mountaineer*, normally on the run between Oban and Fort William, exhanged places with the *Fusilier* and was to be found on the Skye excursion. On 27 September she encountered poor visibility when passing Lismore Lighthouse and ran on to the rocks, becoming a total wreck. The first task of the new decade was to find a replacement.

Second Hand Tonnage

MacBrayne decided in 1890 to keep the *Fusilier* on the popular Oban-Fort William run and bring the *Glencoe* back to Oban yet again for the Skye and Gairloch excursion. By good fortune he had just purchased from a company in Liverpool his first twin screw steamer *Recovery* and it was this new acquisition which he placed on the Portree-Strome Ferry run, duly upgraded and renamed *Flowerdale*. This arrangement only lasted for a year, as MacBrayne commenced purchasing seven second-hand paddle steamers to fulfil his needs. Many came from railway stables and had been well maintained. Unlike the railway companies on the Clyde which had entered a decade of severe if not ruinous competition and were building ever bigger, better and faster steamers, MacBrayne did not have the capital to do this and had to content himself with instituting a veritable museum of veterans.

The little *Handa* was woefully inadequate for the Outer Isles service and so MacBrayne bought the larger *Adela*, renamed her *Staffa* and placed her on the route

When Highland Fisheries withdrew their service from Oban to the Outer Isles MacBrayne immediately stepped in to the breach with the *Clydesdale*; she visited the outlying island of St Kilda on certain occasions and the illustration shows her there

In 1891 the *Flowerdale* sailed round to Oban where her fine sea-going qualities were well utilised on the Outer Isles run; she is seen here at Tobermory

Pier and S. S. „Gael"

The *Gael* was placed in 1891 on the Oban-Skye-Gairloch excursion; here crowds are awaiting her on Tobermory Pier

One of the additions of 1891 was the *Gael* of 1867 which, although originally a Clyde steamer sailing from Campbeltown, had been working out of Weymouth. She was placed, very successfully, on the Oban-Skye-Gairloch excursion, finally displacing the *Glencoe* to Strome Ferry and causing further 'musical chairs'. She also became a very useful winter relief steamer. The *Flowerdale* sailed round to Oban where her fine sea-going qualities were much better utilised on the Outer Isles run; the *Clydesdale*, thus displaced, commenced quite a long association with the Stornoway-Strome Ferry mail run; and the *Lochiel* in turn took over the Portree-Outer Isles-Dunvegan route from the *Staffa*. Meanwhile the Isles route from Oban was becoming overstretched and MacBrayne was able to double the service by transferring the *Staffa* there and so offering a daily sailing.

The *Gael* was not the first elderly paddler to be purchased. An antiquated Clyde steamer dating from 1858, the *Hero*, had been bought in June 1890 to deputise for the *Iona* on the Ardrishaig packet run while the swift steamer was awaiting urgent reboilering. Laid up the following year, she was transformed into a second *Mountaineer* and in 1892 commenced a new career offering short cruises out of Oban. The next addition to the fleet was an essential replacement. The *Islay* had been wrecked in December 1890 in Red Bay, County Antrim and the Stranraer-Larne paddler *Princess Louise*, duly renamed *Islay*, took over the next year.

Meanwhile the doyen of the fleet, the *Inveraray Castle* of 1839, which had survived on the Loch Fyne cargo run for half a century, was unfit for further service and was laid up after the 1890 season. The *Cygnus*, not much her junior at 36 years, was brought in, again from Weymouth, to replace her but proved to be too unwieldy for the run and chartering became the order of the day. Yet again upgrading took place and the 'new swan' appeared in 1892 on the Portree-Strome Ferry mail service as *Brigadier*. The *Glencoe* was transferred to Islay and commenced a stint on the West Loch Tarbert mail run, the only real period in her long career (as *Glencoe*) away from Skye. MacBrayne now had a vessel in hand, the screw steamer *Fingal*, and with her he inaugurated yet another mail service out of Oban - a thrice weekly run to Kilchoan in Ardnamurchan, Coll, Tiree and Bunessan in the Ross of Mull.

1893 saw the commissioning of the *Lovedale* on the Portree-Strome Ferry run. She had been bought as *Great Western* from the Great Western Railway two years before and laid up before renovation. This matching of ship to route lasted for a decade and was the first time that the Skye service could claim a steamer of its own. The *Brigadier* duly became Sound of Mull mailboat to allow the veteran *Pioneer*, having almost reached her half century, to be withdrawn. This provision, on the other hand, did not last beyond a single season: a Southampton-built paddler, the *Albert Edward*, was brought in to Mull and started service for MacBrayne as *Carabinier* in 1894. The *Brigadier* was relegated to spare vessel but her career was destined to be short as she was wrecked off Rodel in Harris late in 1896. It may be recalled that when the Tobermory mail run started in 1881 the cargo service from Glasgow to the Sound of Mull and Loch Sunart ceased: in 1893 it was resuscitated, and extended to Loch

The *Gael* in August 1899 in Loch Scavaig

In 1891 the *Lochiel* took over the Portree-Outer Isles-Dunvegan run from the *Staffa*; she is seen here at Tarbert, Harris around this time

Shipping a Uist Pony. (Copyright)

A Uist pony is being shipped on to the *Lochiel* at Lochmaddy

OCCUPYING ONE DAY.

—:o:—

OBAN to STAFFA and IONA.
'Grenadier' daily at 8 a.m. Cabin (including guide and boat), 15/-.

OBAN to BALLACHULISH for GLENCOE and BACK.
'Fusilier' daily at 6 a.m. and 12.45 p.m. Cabin, 7/6, Steerage, 4/6.

OBAN to FORT WILLIAM and Back.
'Fusilier' daily at 6 a.m. and 12.45 p.m. Cabin, 10/6, Steerage, 6/-.

OBAN to LOCH AWE and Back.
Train daily at 10.5 a.m. and Steamer 'Lochawe' on Loch Awe. Return Tickets issued at Oban Railway Station. Cabin and 1st Class, 9/-; Cabin and 3rd Class, 6/6.

OBAN to CRINAN and Back.
'Chevalier' daily at 8.30 a.m. Cabin (day of issue only), 7/6.

OBAN to CRINAN, ARDRISHAIG and LOCH AWE.
'Chevalier' daily at 8.30 a.m. 'Linnet' on Crinan Canal, Coach to Ford, Steamer 'Lochawe' on Loch Awe and train to Oban. Cabin, Coach, and 1st Class, 15/-.

OBAN to LOCH SUNART and LOCH LINNHE.
Steamer almost daily (see handbill). Coach to Ardgour. 'Fusilier' to Oban. Cabin (including Coach), 18/6.
Oban to Loch Sunart and back. Cabin, 12/-, Steerage, 6/-.

OBAN to TOBERMORY and Back.
'Gael,' 7 a.m., Tuesday, Thursday and Saturday.
'Grenadier,' 8 a.m., Monday, Wednesday, and Friday, returning by alternate steamer. Cabin, 7/6, Steerage, 4/-.

OCCUPYING TWO DAYS.

—:o:—

OBAN to INVERNESS and Back.
'Fusilier' daily at 6 a.m. Returning daily at 7 a.m. via Caledonian Canal. Cabin, 33/-, Steerage, 16/-.

OBAN to GAIRLOCH and Back.
'Gael,' Tuesday, Thursday, and Saturday, at 7 a.m. (via Loch Scavaig for Loch Coruisk on Tuesdays), returning via Sound of Skye on Monday, Wednesday, and Friday, at 6.30 a.m. Cabin, 37/6, Steerage, 22/6.

THE ISLAND ROUTE.
Oban to the Western Isles and back daily from Railway Pier at 6 a.m. Cabin (with good sleeping accommodation), 30/-.

——→✕←——

OCCUPYING THREE DAYS.

—:o:—

Grand Circular Tour.
OBAN, GAIRLOCH, LOCH MAREE, INVERNESS, and CALEDONIAN CANAL.
'Gael' to Gairloch, Tuesday, Thursday, and Saturday at 7 a.m. Coach daily to Achnasheen, train to Inverness, and steamer daily to Oban. Cabin, Coach, and 1st Class, 53/6; (excluding coach and rail), 38/6.
Steamer 'Mabel' on Loch Maree, 5/- extra.

OBAN, PORTREE, STROME FERRY, and INVERNESS.
'Gael' to Portree, Mail Steamer to Strome Ferry, train to Inverness, and steamer to Oban via Caledonian Canal. Cabin and 1st Class, 49/6; (excluding rail), 38/6.

OBAN, DUNVEGAN and PORTREE.
Mail Steamer from Railway Pier, Tuesday, Thursday, and Saturday at 6 a.m. to Dunvegan. 'Lochiel' to Portree, and 'Gael' to Oban. Cabin Fare for round, 40/-.

A timetable card from 1893 featuring the *Columba* and *Iona* and excursions from Oban. This card was featured in Mr Laurence MacBrayne's scrapbook

The *Hero* of 1858 was transformed into a second *Mountaineer* and in 1892 commenced a new career offering short cruises out of Oban; she is seen here in Oban Bay

OBAN, SOUND OF MULL,
ᴬᴺᴰ LOCH SUNART.

Swift THE *Steamer*

"MOUNTAINEER,"
Will Sail from **OBAN** every

MONDAY, WEDNESDAY, ᴬᴺᴰ FRIDAY,
AT 9 A.M., FOR

Craignure, Lochaline, Salen (Mull) Tobermory, Salen (Loch Sunart), and Strontian.

Returning from Strontian same day about 1.30 p.m., and arriving in Oban about 6 p.m.

NOTE.—Return Tickets, Oban to Strontian, Cabin, 12s; available from Corran, Ardgour; Coach Fare, Strontian to Ardgour, 6s 6d.

OFFICIAL GUIDE BOOK, Illustrated, 6d; Cloth Gilt, 1s.

For further particulars as to this and other Tours apply to the owner, DAVID MACBRAYNE, at 119 Hope Street, Glasgow; or to ALEXANDER BROWN, Agent, Steam Packet Office, North Pier, Oban.

AUGUST, 1893.

PRINTED AT THE "OBAN TIMES" OFFICE.

A leaflet from 1893 featuring sailings by the *Mountaineer* (ex *Hero*) from Oban to Loch Sunart in her second season

The Stranraer-Larne paddler *Princess Louise*, duly renamed *Islay*, took over the Islay cargo run in 1891; she is seen here at Port Askaig

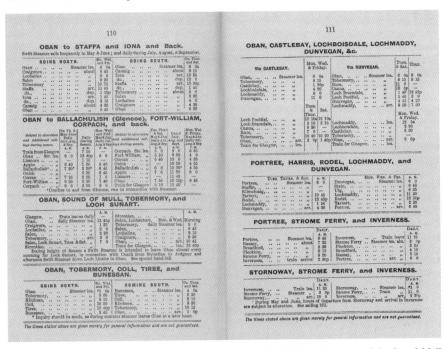

An extract from David MacBrayne's "Summer Tours in Scotland" featuring many of the Royal Mail services in 1894

Leven, with the little *Handa*, a general relief steamer since her removal from the Outer Isles run five years before. Traffic built up so much in fact that five years on the service was doubled when the *Texa* was put on the run as well. This 100 foot cargo steamer had been purchased in 1889.

The final acquisition was the *Sultan* of 1861, another Clyde steamer which had already seen three owners. She was soon altered, shortened and up-graded to emerge in July 1895 as the *Gairlochy*, destined for the Caledonian Canal. The *Glengarry* had just notched up her first fifty years and was demoted from partnering the *Gondolier* to taking the Loch Ness Mail run along with the *Lochness*. At a stroke the through route of swift steamers had been enhanced and the service to the communities on the lochside doubled. The longevity of the steamers working out of Inverness was truly remarkable. One reason for the need for an extra steamer on Loch Ness was the setting up of what was then a 'sunrise' industry at Foyers, the extraction of the very expensive metal aluminium from bauxite, which needed cheap hydro-electric power: the Falls of Foyers provided the ideal location.

Railway Extensions
The main event of the 1890s, other than the purchase of second hand tonnage, was the extension of the railway network. The West Highland Railway, a subsidiary of the North British, thanks to a prodigious feat of engineering in laying track across the desolate Rannoch Moor, reached Fort William in time for the official opening on the day before the "Glorious Twelfth" of 1894. The Lochaber town was *en fête* and the NB had won their west coast terminal between the two railheads at Oban and Strome Ferry. MacBrayne initially opposed the venture but soon learned to cooperate with the WHR. He increased the service from Oban by rostering the *Brigadier* to join the *Fusilier* and *Chevalier* on the Fort William route and even scheduled the *Handa* to sail through the canal from Banavie to Fort Augustus at the foot of Loch Ness. Such extravagance did not last, but traffic did permanently increase and the *Chevalier* was soon able to berth overnight at Fort William rather than Corpach when the line was extended to Banavie a year later.

In November 1897 it was the turn of Highland Railway to open an extension. The original idea had been to make their terminal at Kyle of Lochalsh, just yards across the strait from Skye, but circumstances had dictated otherwise. Now the new section to Kyle was a reality and the *Lovedale* for Portree and the *Gael* on relief duties for Stornoway hanselled the new railhead. Strome Ferry closed and several miles were cut off the steamer journey.

It was into the new century before the final piece of the jigsaw was in place. The WHR completed their uniquely scenic line to Mallaig on the west coast just off the south of Skye in April 1901. The two regular mailboats were in service and the new harbour was duly opened by the *Clydesdale* and *Lovedale*. They now connected with two railheads, operated by two rival companies, although the mail contract was retained by the Highland at Kyle. The all-the-way steamers *Claymore* and *Clansman* now called at Mallaig and abandoned the treacherous approaches to Arisaig, a few miles to the south.

Breakfast 2/-

White Fish and Fresh Herring
or Salmon.
Ham and Eggs, Mutton Chops,
Irish Stew, Sausages, Cold Meats.
Tea and Coffee, Hot Rolls, Preserves.

✛ ✛ ✛

Luncheon 2/-

Cold Roast Beef, Corned Beef, Lamb,
and Hot Potatoes.
Cheese, Biscuits, and Oat Cakes.

Hot Soup served on s.s. Loch-Awe."

✛ ✛ ✛

Dinner 2/6* and 3/-

Soups, White Fish or Salmon.
Roast Beef, Corned Beef, Roast Lamb,
and Mint Sauce.
Boiled Mutton and Caper Sauce,
Chicken, Tongues.
Green Peas, Hot Potatoes,
Vegetables (various).
Cheese, Biscuits, Oatcakes, and Salad.

Sweets served on s.s. "Claymore," "Clansman."
"Cavalier," and Staffa and Iona Steamer.

✻ *Dinner—2/6 on board Glasgow & Ardrishaig, and*
Crinan & Oban, Steamers, 3/- on other Steamers.

Tea 2/-

Hot Fish, Cold Meats, and Boiled Eggs.
Toast, Fancy Bread, Biscuits,
and Preserves.

✛ ✛ ✛

Plain Tea 1/-

Toast, Fancy Bread, Biscuits,
and Preserves.

✛ ✛ ✛

Sundries.

Cup of Tea, with Biscuit, - - 6d.
Cup of Coffee, with Biscuit, - - 6d.
Sandwich, - - - 4d. and 6d.
Aerated Waters, - - 6d. per Bot.
Beer and Porter, - - 6d. per Bot.
Whisky, Rum, and Gin, 6d. per Gl.
Brandy, - - - 9d. per Gl.

CIGARS, CIGARETTES, CUT TOBACCOES, &c.

✛ ✛ ✛

Wines

Of every description and of the best
vintages kept on board.

See Special Wine List.

A menu card from 1896 featuring the various meals on offer. Only the *Lochawe* offered hot soup for luncheon and only certain vessels had sweets as the alternative to biscuits and cheese

At the end of the nineteenth century the longevity of the swift steamers working out of Inverness was truly remarkable; seen here are, from left to right, the *Gondolier* (1866), the *Gairlochy* (1861) and the *Glengarry* (1844)

38

The *Gael* lying at Strome Ferry while relieving on the Portree or Stornoway mail run; the pier closed to regular traffic when the railhead at Kyle of Lochalsh was opened in 1897

On 2 November 1897 the *Lovedale* for Portree (close to the camera) and the *Gael* on relief duties for Stornoway hanselled the new railhead at Kyle of Lochalsh; the *Gael* also carried out a celebration cruise

Jubilee

Before this final extension, however, David Hutcheson & Co/David MacBrayne had just celebrated their jubilee of service to the West Highlands and Islands. A comparison of the main routes of 1851 and 1901 in the summer season indicates how comprehensive the advances had been over the period.

ROUTE	1851	1901
Glasgow-Ardrishaig	*P.S.Pioneer*	*P.S.Columba*
Ardrishaig-Glasgow	-	*P.S.Iona*
Ardrishaig-Crinan	Two trackboats	*S.S.Linnet*
Corpach-Crinan	*P.S.Shandon*	*P.S.Chevalier*
Inverness-Banavie	*P.S.Edinburgh Castle*	*P.S.Gondolier*
Banavie-Inverness	-	*P.S.Gairlochy*
Inverness-Invergordon	*P.S.Curlew*	-
Loch Ness Mail	-	*P.S.Glengarry*
Loch Ness Mail (2)	-	*P.S.Lochness*
Islay-West Loch Tarbert	-	*P.S.Glencoe*
Oban-Outer Isles (MWF)	-	*S.S.Flowerdale*
Oban-Outer Isles (TThS)	-	*S.S.Staffa*
Tobermory-Oban	-	*P.S.Carabinier*
Oban-Staffa-Iona	*P.S.Dolphin*	*P.S.Grenadier*
Oban-Skye-Gairloch	-	*P.S.Gael*
Oban-Fort William	-	*P.S.Fusilier*
Oban-Short Cruises/Fort William	-	*P.S.Mountaineer*
Oban-Bunessan	-	*S.S.Fingal*
Portree-Outer Isles	-	*S.S.Lochiel*
Portree-Kyle-Mallaig	-	*P.S.Lovedale*
Stornoway-Kyle-Mallaig	-	*S.S.Clydesdale*
Glasgow-Stornoway (Mon)	*P.S. Duntroon Castle*	*S.S.Clansman*
Glasgow-Stornoway (Thu)	(Portree only)	*S.S.Claymore*
Glasgow-Inverness (Mon)	*P.S.Lapwing*	*S.S.Cavalier*
Glasgow-Inverness (Thu)	*P.S.Cygnet*	*S.S.Ethel*
Glasgow-Islay	-	*P.S.Islay*
Glasgow-Inveraray	-	*S.S.Aggie*
Glasgow-Loch Sunart/Leven (Mon)	-	*S.S.Handa*
Glasgow-Loch Sunart/Leven (Fri)	-	*S.S.Texa*

Clyde Competition

As had happened twice before, the story is carried forward because of happenings on the Clyde. A new century (and a new monarch) brought a new mode of propulsion and in 1901 the first commercial turbine steamer *King Edward* came into service, followed by the *Queen Alexandra* the following year. The movement of these ships was so smooth and so fast that the competition with the *Columba* and *Iona* was very intense and one-sided, especially from 1902 when the "*Edward*" opened up a new route to Inveraray. To add to his woes, MacBrayne had to suffer the loss of the *Islay* by stranding near Port Ellen in July 1902. His response was first of all to buy, in September, a handsome, but slow, cross-channel steamer whose name he changed to

Glendale. Then he changed the *Iona's* roster in 1903 to allow a double express service from Ardrishaig at 5.45 a.m. and 1 p.m. to the railhead at Wemyss Bay (and, in the morning, Greenock, Prince's Pier) with fast train connections to and from the city. In addition the *Grenadier*, the normal winter boat on the Ardrishaig run, remained on the Clyde for the season to supplement the sailings between the Kyles of Bute and Glasgow as the *Iona* no longer sailed up river. This led to a further change round of vessels in the West Highlands: the Staffa and Iona run was taken by the *Gael* and her place on the Gairloch excursion by the *Glendale*.

New Tonnage at Last
The replacement of the *Islay* is indirectly caught up with the other major event of 1902, namely that at the age of 88, David MacBrayne admitted to full partnership his two sons, David Hope and Laurence. They had actually been employees throughout their lives but only now were each given 25% of the share of the business. They were able to relieve their father of the day-to-day running of the firm. A change in attitude was immediately apparent and new tonnage was ordered for the first time in fifteen years. Ornithological names were revived and a new screw steamer *Lapwing* entered service in 1903. The unpretentious yard which was Scott's of Bowling replaced Thomson's of Clydebank in the Company's thinking: the *Lapwing* was utilitarian without any of the gilt apparent in the older vessels, economical but hardy; she took over from the *Staffa* on the Islands run from Oban. The *Staffa* was displaced to her old run, the Tarbert and Lochmaddy service from Portree, and the *Lochiel* could then be spared for the Portree-Mallaig service. This, then, allowed the *Lovedale* to remain on the Glasgow-Islay route, where she had gone soon after the loss of the *Islay*.

1903 was the peak year of services offered by David MacBrayne. The following year the *Grenadier* was only needed on the Clyde during Glasgow Fair fortnight, the *Gael* returned to the Oban-Gairloch run and the *Glendale* was only needed for Staffa and Iona when the *Grenadier* was away, spending the rest of the season spare in Oban Bay. For the rest of the decade the priority was to replace outdated tonnage with more suitable, if less sumptuous, vessels. The *Clydesdale*, for example, was over forty years old and not considered acceptable for such an important rôle as the Stornoway mailboat. The MacBrayne family went to Inglis of Pointhouse for a replacement and they created an outstanding vessel, the *Sheila*, the fleet's first triple expansion steamship and for over two decades a staunch favourite of the Lewis folk. She took up service in March 1904.

Later that same year came the *Plover*, a quasi-sister of the *Lapwing*, to take over from the ageing *Flowerdale* on the Barra run from Oban. Finally the *Cygnet* was launched. Unlike her sisters, she did not require sleeping accommodation as she was to be used mainly in the Loch Fyne cargo trade. For the first time since the *Mary Jane* became *Glencoe* in 1875 the Inveraray cargo run had a daily departure from Glasgow, in direct opposition to the Loch Fyne merchants' *Minard Castle*. Her opposite number was the *Texa*, whose Friday Glasgow-Loch Sunart run had been discontinued previously. This was a temporary expedient, as the *Brenda*, a chubby vessel capable of negotiating the Crinan Canal, was built in late 1904 to be the

It was a tradition for steamers' crews to pose periodically for the cameraman; here the officers of the *Iona* are seen on board

MacBrayne's response to competition in 1903 was to change the *Iona*'s roster to allow a double express run from Ardrishaig to Wemyss Bay; this meant that at lunchtime the *Columba* (right) and *Iona* would be seen together at Ardrishaig

In 1903 the *Grenadier*, the normal winter boat on the Ardrishaig run, remained on the Clyde for the season; she is seen here at Ardrishaig in her original condition

The MacBrayne family went to Inglis of Pointhouse for a replacement for the old *Clydesdale* as Stornoway mailboat - the *Sheila*, seen here leaving Mallaig

43

In 1904 the *Plover* took over from the ageing *Flowerdale* on the Barra run from Oban; she is seen here on the Clyde on trials

In 1904 the *Texa* sailed to Loch Fyne on alternate days to the *Cygnet*; she is seen here approaching Ardrishaig

Handa's consort on the Loch Sunart and Loch Leven cargo service.

The 1904 season was the *Lovedale's* last, as she was considered fit only for the scrapheap. Her place on the Glasgow-Islay route was taken by the spare *Glendale*. Islay saw another new vessel in 1905 - a second *Pioneer*. Unlike the other paddle steamers in the fleet, she had a distinctly modern feel about her, being plated up to the bow, with her single funnel well forward (but curiously with the bridge still aft) and the top of her paddlebox flush with her promenade deck. She gave yeoman service on the route from Port Ellen and Port Askaig to West Loch Tarbert, calling at Gigha and Jura respectively. This was the cue for the *Glencoe's* transfer back to Skye, although by now of course the mailboat sailed to Kyle of Lochalsh and Mallaig rather than Strome Ferry and gave a cruise to Loch Coruisk in the heart of the Cuillins twice a week. The *Lochiel* once again turned north rather than south on leaving Portree as she made for Tarbert, Lochmaddy and Dunvegan. The ultimate consequence was that the *Staffa*, dating from 1861, became spare.

Sadly Islay did not see much of the *Glendale* as she was wrecked off the Mull of Kintyre in July 1905. Fortunately the MacBrayne firm had just built a new *Clydesdale*, virtually a repeat of the *Cavalier*, for the Glasgow-Inverness run. Her presence on the Inverness run, however, was not essential and so she was transferred to the Islay cargo route almost immediately following the *Glendale's* loss.

The Pre-eminence of MacBrayne
The *Clydesdale* was the last of the 1903-5 building spree. With the company set fair for the future with seven new ships in the fleet and several of the aged vessels withdrawn, Laurence MacBrayne sold his 25% share to his elder brother in December, while on 1 January 1906 a private limited company, with David Hope MacBrayne as Chairman, was incorporated. David MacBrayne himself retired at the same time but retained a 50% share in the ships and still visited the office in 119 Hope Street, Glasgow, once every day: he was to live for one year only, his death occurring on 26 January 1907 at the age of 92. His shares were then transferred to David MacBrayne Ltd.

It is difficult to overestimate the contribution David MacBrayne made to the welfare of the West Highlands and Islands of Scotland. Even in the days of the Burns empire he was active in the promotion of sailings in the area and when the Messrs Burns sold out in 1851 he became a partner of the new firm. Gradually his influence became greater and greater as David Hutcheson edged towards retirement. The fleet grew from eight to over thirty and the company's sphere of influence expanded out of all recognition, with over a hundred ports of call either by pier or ferry. His ships were renowned for their pre-eminently sumptuous fittings and his officers and crews for their Highland courtesy and their superlative skill in negotiating all sorts of difficult waters in at times tempestuous conditions. Although in his latter years perhaps a touch conservative - understandably - he never stood still and if he was not always completely proactive he always responded immediately and positively to a challenge. His management style probably leaned rather towards benign despotism but he was a much-loved old gentleman nevertheless.

Islay saw two new vessels in 1905 - one was the second *Pioneer*; she is seen here in an atmospheric picture at Port Askaig, sharing the pier with a puffer

MacBrayne's had just built a new *Clydesdale* for the Glasgow-Inverness run in 1905 but she was transferred to the Islay cargo run almost immediately following the loss of the *Glendale*; in this picture she is berthed at Kyle

46

A portrait of David Hope MacBrayne who became Chairman of the private limited company on 1 January 1906

One of the first innovations of David MacBrayne Ltd was to introduce an omnibus between Fort William and North Ballachulish; their first new 'bus was a chain-driven 14-seater Albion

Motor Buses and Motor Vessels

One of the first innovations of the new company in 1906 was to introduce an omnibus between Fort William and North Ballachulish. The first vehicle was second-hand, bought from the Isle of Wight - a German Daimler, rack driven and seating about 35 - while the first new vehicle was a chain-driven 14-seater Albion. The omnibus linked Fort William with the trains to Oban across Loch Leven at Ballachulish. This area round Loch Leven was just developing, thanks to the building of an aluminium factory, like the one at Falls of Foyers, near the new village of Kinlochleven at the head of the loch. As there was no road along the north of the loch and that on the south bank was not much better than a track, the main transport was by sea and from late 1905 the shopkeepers ran a small launch to Ballachulish. Soon after a channel was dredged MacBrayne's stepped in and provided a service, from November 1907, by the small paddler *Mountaineer* and then by a ship specially bought in for the run.

This was the *Win*, a 65 foot launch built in London and propelled by an internal combustion engine fuelled by paraffin from Gardner's of Manchester. Given the name *Comet* after the first commercial Clyde steamer - appropriately since she was the first motor vessel in the fleet - she was no beauty but, after being commissioned in January 1908, she served the Company for forty years. She must be deemed a success. A purpose-built motor vessel, the *Scout*, was also employed on the route. She sailed up to Fort William in winter in lieu of the Oban steamer: by now there was a connection via the new Ballachulish railway line with Oban.

MacBrayne's third motor vessel, the *Lochinvar*, was altogether different and at almost 150 feet one of the larger members of the fleet. Hardly a graceful craft, she made up for her lack of looks by a dependability which served the Mull islanders well for half a century on her daily voyage from Tobermory to Oban. She was in fact built in 1908 as the replacement for the *Carabinier*, which was sold for scrap.

Edwardian Twilight

Meanwhile, in complete contrast, a ship which has been described as a 'glorious anachronism' had joined the fleet in 1907. The first vessel to exceed 1000 gross tons - the old *Cygnet* of 1848 was just over 100 - the *Chieftain* was like a millionaire's yacht with her glorious clipper bow and her overall graceful lines. By now the Glasgow-Stornoway run was a Mecca for tourists and a new grander ship was required to partner the *Claymore*, although she still had to be able to handle the essential cargo which was carried. The *Chieftain*, then, duly replaced the *Clansman* although the smaller more economical ship maintained the winter service until she was withdrawn in 1909.

The rest of the Edwardian years saw David MacBrayne Ltd undergo a limited programme of fleet replacement. In 1907 the *Lochiel*, on the Outer Isles run from Skye, ran aground off Portree and could not be salvaged. The Company went to Scott's of Bowling for a replacement and they produced a rather handsome vessel, a second *Lochiel*. Always ready to innovate, MacBrayne's gave her a gyromechanism to try to cut down rolling in the exposed passage to the Hebrides. She was in fact

The first paraffin-fuelled motor vessel in the fleet, the *Comet*, was specially bought in for the new run between Ballachulish and Kinlochleven, starting in January 1908. Later she was transferred to the Lochgoilhead mail run; she is seen here approaching Gourock in March 1930

MacBrayne's first purpose-built motor vessel, the *Scout*, was also commissioned on the Loch Leven service; she is seen here at Kinlochleven along with the *Loch Leven Queen* (right)

A 'glorious anachronism' joined MacBrayne's fleet in 1907 to partner the *Claymore* on the Glasgow-Stornoway run; the *Chieftain* is seen here in Oban Bay

The *Dirk*, distinguished by having a very tall funnel out of proportion to her hull, succeeded the *Lochiel* on the Oban-Tiree-Bunessan run in 1909; she is seen here in Oban Bay

placed on the Tiree-Bunessan run from Oban because of the complaints about the inadequacy of the *Fingal* and it was the old *Staffa* which went to Portree. The *Fingal* became spare and was often to be found on the cargo run on the Clyde. A further smallish screw ship was added in 1909, again from Scott's of Bowling. The *Dirk*, distinguished by having a very tall funnel out of proportion to her hull, succeeded the *Lochiel* on the Tiree run, the *Lochiel* in turn was transferred to the Isles run from Oban, the *Lapwing* to Portree-Harris-Dunvegan and the *Staffa* was scrapped.

The Company often had to resort to chartering at crucial times like the annual autumn livestock movements from the islands or when the overhaul schedule was being stretched. One little cargo ship frequently chartered was the *Nellie* and MacBrayne's actually purchased her outright in 1908, renaming her *Staffa* when the name became available two years later and placing her largely on the cargo run to Loch Leven, where traffic was increasing. The *Handa* once again became spare.

The last new build of the period, in 1910, also turned out to be MacBrayne's last paddle steamer. She was a replacement for the *Mountaineer*, which at over 50 had reached the end of her useful life. Also named *Mountaineer*, the new ship was a product, like the *Pioneer*, of Inglis of Pointhouse, and like her she had very small paddle wheels, although she could easily be distinguished as her promenade deck was not continued to the bow. Like her predecessor she was used for cruises out of Oban and for supplementary runs to Fort William.

Loch Leven still continued to occupy the directors of David MacBrayne Ltd. To oppose the *Comet* and *Scout* a group of local Kinlochleven businessmen, who already owned the launch *Cona*, had purchased in 1908 a vessel which had started life as a cross-river ferry in Glasgow Harbour - *Clutha No 12*. Renamed *Loch Leven Queen*, she attracted a fair number of passengers despite charging higher fares than the mighty MacBrayne's. Competition came to an end, however, in 1911 when MacBrayne's bought over the two ships. The following year they transferred the *Loch Leven Queen* to the Loch Ness mail run in place of the old *Lochness*, which was scrapped after 59 years' service. She too was duly renamed *Lochness*. The *Scout* herself suffered a disastrous fire aboard in August 1913, not perhaps surprising when one considers the primitive method of lighting the paraffin to fuel her engine. She was unfit for further service, her place being taken the following year by a small screw steamer of Irish origin, the *Countess of Mayo*.

One further interest accruing to David MacBrayne Ltd was the goodwill of the services to and from Lochgoilhead on the Clyde on the demise of the Lochgoil & Inveraray Steamboat Company in 1912. The old Lochgoilhead steamer *Edinburgh Castle* was withdrawn after the 1913 season and MacBrayne steamers assisted in plugging the gap, both the *Mountaineer* and *Chevalier* appearing on the route. In 1914, however, *M.V. Comet* was transferred permanently from Loch Leven to provide a daily service all the year round.

The *Loch Leven Queen* was transferred to the Loch Ness mail run in 1912 and was renamed *Lochness*, the second in the fleet; her crew posed for this photograph

Captain Lachlan McTavish of the *Columba*

The Great War

During this period the tourist trade actually declined and traffic numbers started to dwindle. The first victim was the *Maree* on Loch Maree which ceased to sail after the 1911 season. It hardly needs to be said that the Great War greatly and immediately accelerated the process. War was actually declared on 4 August 1914 and within a week MacBrayne's services were affected: the second Ardrishaig mail steamer *Iona* was no longer required and the Oban excursion programme was curtailed. On 1 July 1915, however, the repercussions were more obvious when a boom was erected between the Cloch Lighthouse and Dunoon, thus effectively cutting the Firth of Clyde in two. Through sailings to the Highlands and Islands were hardly affected but the Ardrishaig mail service had to be given from Wemyss Bay, south of the boom, and by the *Iona*, the *Columba* being laid up. The sailings of the *Linnet* on the Crinan Canal and *Lochawe* on Loch Awe ceased, the latter permanently. Sailings between Oban and Skye and Gairloch by the *Gael* were likewise never revived after the 1914 season.

Few MacBrayne steamers were requisitioned by the Admiralty, one notable exception being the *Grenadier*, which as *HMS Grenade* spent three years from July 1916 minesweeping in the North Sea. The railway steamers on the Clyde, on the other hand, were almost all 'called up' and several MacBrayne ships were chartered by the railway companies or their subsidiaries to maintain essential services. The *Chevalier*, *Fusilier*, *Gael*, *Glencoe*, *Lochinvar* and *Mountaineer* all appeared on Clyde rosters.

Meanwhile in August 1915, in an attempt to effect economies and to provide the minimum service really needed by the coast communities during the emergency, all Clyde cargo services were amalgamated into a new company, Clyde Cargo Steamers Ltd. The daily MacBrayne cargo runs to Loch Fyne were included in the deal, and, although the Company was no longer responsible for the service, ships like the *Cygnet*, *Fingal* and *Texa* were still used on it quite frequently.

Services in the West Highlands were pruned to the bare minimum. The *Sheila*, for example, served both Portree and Stornoway from Mallaig and Kyle of Lochalsh while the *Plover* alone remained on the Outer Isles services she had previously shared with the *Lapwing* and *Lochiel*. She contrived to do this by working alternately out of Oban and Kyle. Mull was served by one vessel only - the *Dirk* until June 1917 and then the *Lochinvar* - while the *Pioneer* remained at Islay for the duration of the war. Excursions of a sort were still offered out of Oban, rather unexpectedly, by the *Mountaineer* for the first two years and the *Glencoe* thereafter. All the fleet was eventually painted in naval grey.

A Decade of Decline

On the Clyde the *Columba* was laid up, apart from a very few weeks in the summer of 1916, until the 1917 season, when she returned to the fray as her older sister was on semi-permanent charter to The Caledonian Steam Packet Company. It was in 1917 also that two of MacBrayne's screw steamers were requisitioned by the Admiralty. Neither the *Dirk* nor the *Lochiel* survived: both were blown up in 1918.

Few MacBrayne steamers were requisitioned by the Admiralty, one notable exception being the *Grenadier*, which as HMS *Grenade* spent three years minesweeping in the North Sea

The *Fusilier* and *Mountaineer* on charter to The Caledonian Steam Packet Co seen off Millport, Isle of Cumbrae

Several MacBrayne veterans appeared on Clyde rosters during the Great War; the *Chevalier* is seen here, in a photograph discovered by William Lind, at Kilchattan Bay, Bute, in 1919, on charter to the CSP

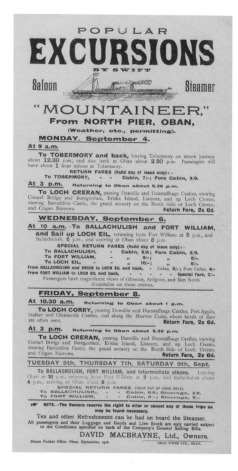

Excursions of a sort were still offered out of Oban during the Great War; the illustration shows the handbill for the *Mountaineer* in September 1916

With the cuts in service on the home front several ships became redundant. The Kinlochleven cargo vessel *Staffa* and the Inverness steamer *Clansman* (the *Ethel* had been thus renamed in 1910) left the fleet in April and May 1916 respectively, while the following year all the spare cargo boats were sold - the *Fingal* in January, the *Handa* in May and the *Texa* in August. In addition the two Loch Leven craft *Countess of Mayo* and *Cona* had left the fleet by the summer. At the beginning of 1917 the *Lapwing*, relieving at Oban, had run aground; she was salved and eventually commenced a new life as *Cowal* for Clyde Cargo Steamers.

The Armistice was at last signed on 11 November 1918. David MacBrayne Ltd had lost or sold ten of his fleet, one (the *Lochawe*) was permanently laid up and others were still chartered to provide essential Clyde sailings. David Hope MacBrayne himself had suffered personal tragedy when his wife died and his only son was killed in combat. The Directors had to cut their cloth to suit the changed circumstances but their losses were mitigated by the fact that the public's appetite for Grand Circular Tours and the more exotic excursions had waned, the country was plagued for nearly a decade by industrial unrest and road transport had made great inroads into routes previously served by sea.

On the Clyde the Ardrishaig-Wemyss Bay express was not revived but from 1922 the *Iona* found alternative seasonal employment giving an excursion from Glasgow to Lochgoilhead and Arrochar as a supplement to the *Comet's* mail runs. A fire completely destroyed the *Gairlochy* at Fort Augustus late in 1919. The *Linnet* had resumed that year as had the *Chevalier* from Crinan to Oban. In 1920, however, the *Fusilier* took over the Crinan run, followed by the *Mountaineer* in 1923. The veteran *Chevalier*, now well over 50 years old, was thereafter confined to occasional excursion and relief sailings on the Clyde and was laid up in Bowling Harbour for most of the year. The Oban-based excursion steamers were therefore cut from five to three, the *Grenadier*, returned safely from service under the white ensign, still looking after Staffa and Iona while the *Fusilier* and *Mountaineer* served Crinan and Fort William between them, the *Gael's* Skye excursion not being renewed.

Oban suffered in other ways too. The Outer Isles service, cut during the war from three schedules to one, was at least now operated by two ships, but only one called at Oban. The *Plover* was now based at Kyle of Lochalsh and Mallaig and met up with the Oban boat at Lochboisdale in South Uist, where an interchange of passengers, goods and mail could be effected. With neither the *Lapwing* nor the *Lochiel* available, the mantle of the Oban-Coll-Tiree-Barra-Lochboisdale roster fell on the *Cygnet*, the third of the utiliarian trio of the 1900s. Before she could serve on the Islands route she had to be fitted with sleeping accommodation; she also acquired a mainmast. The Oban-Tiree-Bunessan service was never renewed after the war so that Mull had to make do solely with the Sound of Mull mailboat *Lochinvar* and Tiree with the *Cygnet*.

Oban was also an important port of call for the Glasgow-Inverness steamers. Since the withdrawal of the *Clansman* ex *Ethel* the service was entrusted to the *Cavalier* alone but as road transport had overtaken the century-old sea route even she was sold in 1919

From 1922 the *Iona* found seasonal employment giving an excursion from Glasgow to Lochgoilhead and Arrochar; she is seen here at Douglas Pier on the west side of Loch Goil near its head

In the 1920s the veteran *Chevalier* was confined to occasional excursion and relief sailings on the Clyde; she is seen here approaching Rothesay one Glasgow Fair with full complement

and the service through the Caledonian Canal axed. Finally, the *Chieftain*, altogether too grand and uneconomic for the post-war scene, was sold in June 1919. Meanwhile the *Claymore's* roster changed: she now left Glasgow every ten days or so on the "Skye and Mainland" cargo route carrying cruise passengers in addition, although Stornoway still remained a port of call on some voyages. The Admiralty, to compensate for MacBrayne's war losses, assigned to the Company the Channel Islands vessel *Devonia*: she was placed on the Glasgow-Stornoway route, but with cargo only; she was renamed *Lochiel* one year into her service. Oban therefore experienced a total shortfall of seven passenger vessels in 1920 when compared with 1914.

David MacBrayne Ltd gradually expanded their omnibus services since the small beginnings in 1906. 1911 had seen a service start between Inverness and Glenurqhart because of another omnibus service in opposition to the Loch Ness mail steamer: this challenge was eventually overcome. The following year a service had started between Fort William and Inverness and in 1913 to Ardrishaig from both Oban and Inveraray. By 1919 Loch Leven was totally bereft of steamers and the *Lochness* was brought back from Fort Augustus to fill the gap. By 1923, however, she too was declared redundant and, since there had been a considerable improvement in the road system round the loch, 'bus transport was substituted - the steamer returned to Loch Ness.

The Company never really recovered from the Great War. The serious national economic position with inflation at previously unknown levels, and the abundance of industrial strikes causing, fundamentally, lack of money 'coming up the gangway' meant that the climate of improvement and growth which had been so evident since 1851 could not be achieved. Many of the fleet were ancient and the newer vessels had not been built to the same high standards as those from the nineteenth century. The *Cygnet's* being entrusted to the Outer Isles run from Oban was the cause of most complaints - even reaching Parliament in Westminster - but that was merely symptomatic of the malaise affecting the whole operation.

Disaster
Then in 1927 triple disaster struck. In the early hours of New Year's Day the *Sheila*, inward bound from Stornoway and under the command of a relief master, ran aground well off course when attempting to make her regular ferry call at Applecross. Fortunately there were no fatalities but the ship herself was a total loss. The *Clydesdale* was immediately transferred to the Stornoway mail run, her place at Islay being taken by the Stornoway cargo boat *Lochiel*. Her place in turn was filled by chartered vessels. Then in late March the *Chevalier*, while relieving on the winter Greenock-Ardrishaig service, ran aground off Barmore Island just north of Tarbert following a paddle wheel jam caused by a broken float. Although she was refloated and able to proceed to Greenock the Company decided that, at 61 years, she was not worth repairing and had her scrapped.

A more crucial loss came in September when a disastrous fire broke out on board the *Grenadier* as she lay at Oban's North Pier overnight, killing three of her crew,

The *Cygnet*'s being entrusted to the Outer Isles run from Oban was the cause of most complaints reaching MacBrayne's; she is seen here in her post-war condition

In the early hours of New Year's Day 1927 the Stornoway mail steamer *Sheila* ran aground well off course when attempting to make her regular ferry call at Applecross

In late March 1927 the *Chevalier*, while relieving on the Greenock-Ardrishaig mail service, ran aground off Barmore Island just north of Tarbert

A disastrous fire broke out on the *Grenadier* at Oban in Septmber 1927; she subsequently sank but was eventually raised and towed to the Clyde for scrapping

including her Master. She sank at her berth but was eventually raised and taken to the Clyde. Like the other swift steamer of a bygone age she was considered beyond economic repair and she too was broken up - at Ardrossan. For the 1928 season the Staffa and Iona excursion was entrusted to the *Fusilier*, the *Iona* was brought back to Oban after an absence of over forty years to look after the Fort William traffic while her place on the Lochgoihead and Arrochar was taken by the Clyde paddler *Lord of the Isles* under charter.

The decision was also taken to withdraw the *Glengarry* from Loch Ness at the end of the season on 27 October. Remarkably still driven by her original steeple engine, she was at 83 years of age the oldest steamship in the world. Sadly, preservation was not the order of the day in the 1920s and she was broken up almost immediately. *S.S. Lochness* took over but she too was withdrawn in September 1928 and scrapped. The *Gondolier* was now the only vessel working Loch Ness and the Caledonian Canal.

A Rescue Package
If David MacBrayne Ltd was suffering from hard times earlier, and David Hope himself at a personal level too, by 1928 the Directors were in the depths of despair. The earlier problems persisted and were compounded by the woeful inadequacy of the *Clydesdale* on the Stornoway mail run and the complete unsuitability of the 13-knot *Fusilier* for the Iona excursion in summer and the Ardrishaig mail service in winter. The crisis finally broke when David Hope MacBrayne withdrew the Company's tender for the mail contract. The Government sought applications to take over but without success. After long debates in the House a rescue package was put in place. Sir Alfred Read, Chairman and Managing Director of Coast Lines Ltd and Sir Josiah Stamp, President of the LMS Railway Company, offered to acquire the fleet and goodwill of David MacBrayne Ltd in the name of their two companies. The cost was a mere £77 000. Prime Minster Stanley Baldwin readily accepted this lifeline and a contract was drawn up. The name of the new company was David MacBrayne (1928) Ltd. It came into being on 1 November 1928 with Sir Alfred as Chairman and MD. The new Board comprised, as well as the Chairman, Sir Josiah Stamp as Vice Chairman, Sir Alexander Gracie, representing the interests of the LMS Railway, Lt-Col Norman MacLeod, representing Government interests, and James W Ratledge. Mr H T Leith continued as General Manager, a post he had held since 1923. David Hope MacBrayne retired, at the age of 66. For the first time since 1851 there was no MacBrayne in the Company, but the two leading figures - protagonists in the wider commercial sense - brought their very considerable expertise, drive and, not least, political connections, to the aid of the new Company and it survived. One other important change took place at this time, namely that while the day to day running of the fleet manifestly was still controlled from Glasgow, the strategic planning took place in London. It was to be almost a century before this was completely reversed. Incidentally, David MacBrayne (1928) Ltd obtained air powers at this time but they were never exercised directly.

The Government insisted that to win the mail contract the new firm had to build at least four new vessels within two years and that fares and freight charges should be lowered. To effect this it was obvious that at least two ancient routes had to close. The *Gondolier* was permitted to continue on the Loch Ness mail run throughout the 1928/29 winter - an unusual duty for her - but after that it was axed. 'Buses took over between Inverness and Foyers and Inverness and Fort Augustus, carrying passengers, mail and parcels. The Company started a novel venture at the same time when they bought a lorry to transport goods and livestock along the latter route.

Speed was considered to be of the essence and the leisurely and colourful sail through the Canal from Ardrishaig in connection with the Glasgow and Oban steamers was considered unsuitable and uneconomic. The quaint little *Linnet* was sold and became a club house in the Gareloch on the Clyde. At the same time the Crinan-Oban leg of the Royal Route was discontinued, the *Mountaineer* being able subsequently to offer a greater variety of cruises out of Oban. A 'bus took passengers between Ardrishaig and Oban as part of the "Tour Majestic". In addition the charter of the *Lord of the Isles* was not renewed and the Company's interests in Lochgoilhead were once again confined to the *Comet's* sailings.

Following the removal of the *Lochiel* from the Stornoway cargo run to take over the Islay service in 1927, expensive chartering had been taking place to fill the gap and one of the first acts of the new Company was to procure a permanent replacement. It is not surprising that this came from Coast Lines, who were able to release one of their older vessels launched in 1891 as *Grouse* but now known as *Denbigh Coast*: she took up service in May 1929. Since its inception Hutcheson/MacBrayne had indulged in a certain amount of systematic nomenclature - bird names, names ending in *-dale* and, most prominently, names ending in *-ier* or *-eer*. To confirm the Company's new status a new system was required: from now and for some 25 years every new ship was to have a single name beginning with *Loch*. The *Denbigh Coast* was thus renamed *Lochdunvegan*.

A New Generation
The first of the new ships specified in the mail contract took up service on the Stornoway-Kyle-Mallaig mail service on 1 August 1929. The imposing *Lochness* was a huge improvement on the *Clydesdale* and immediately won the approval of the Lewis islanders. Though her accommodation was not lavish it was comfortable and her speed of 14 knots, though not exactly fast, was more than adequate for her service. The *Lochness* was actually the last steamship built for the Company: rather than burning coal she used the cleaner and cheaper oil as fuel, obtaining it from a large stock tank at Kyle of Lochalsh specially erected for her. The *Clydesdale* was able to return to Islay and the *Lochiel* became spare cargo vessel for use in relieving and for the transport of livestock. To project a new image, incidentally, all the new contracted ships were painted grey and even the *Columba* and *Claymore* had to don the alien paint. The public reaction was fierce and the experiment soon ended ignominiously.

In October 1929 further new tonnage entered the fleet, though she was not part of the Government contract. This was the *Lochshiel*, a modern cargo motor ship with the machinery aft. She was commissioned as a replacement for the *Brenda*

When the *Glengarry* and *Lochness* were withdrawn from service at the end of the 1927 and 1928 seasons respectively the *Gondolier* was the only vessel working Loch Ness and the Caledonian Canal; she is seen here in the locks at Fort Augustus in 1934

David MacBrayne (1928) Ltd started a novel venture when they bought a lorry to transport goods and livestock between Inverness and Fort Augustus

The imposing *Lochness* took up service on the Stornoway-Kyle-Mallaig mail service in August 1929; she is seen here in her original grey-hulled condition at Kyle of Lochalsh

The *Lochshiel*, a modern cargo motor ship with the machinery aft, was commissioned in 1929 on the Loch Sunart and Loch Leven cargo run; she is seen here approaching Tobermory in July 1950

on the Loch Sunart and Loch Leven cargo run. Apart from being more economical, she was much more efficient than her predecessor and again was instrumental in assisting the Company to make ends meet. The older ship was broken up.

The second and third of the new ships specified by the Government were genuine sisters, the *Lochearn* and the *Lochmor*. They were both destined for the Outer Isles, the former as a replacement for the *Cygnet* out of Oban and the latter in lieu of the *Plover* out of Kyle and Mallaig. The Oban-based ship was known as the Inner Isles mailboat while the other was the Outer Isles mail steamer. Cynics described them as "a pair of models bought at a toy shop" but, though undoubtedly ugly when compared with the traditional steamers, they were very functional and their internal accommodation far exceeded anything which had gone before. They did not reach the Company's expectations for speed, however, and just over 9 knots on the voyage to the Outer Isles was relatively tedious. When the new pair took up service late in the summer of 1930 the much-criticised *Cygnet* was sold for scrap and the *Plover* retained as spare vessel. The reliance on diesel power must surely have been a direct result of the influence of Sir Alfred Read, Coast Lines having already gone down that path. The choice of shipyard was not insignificant either - it was Ardrossan Dockyard, owned by Coast Lines.

1930 saw the last of one of the great favourites of all time in the West Highlands, *S.S.Claymore*. She had been threatened with withdrawal after the previous season but was reprieved for one year, the problem being that she urgently needed reboilering and was already almost 50 years old. Plans to convert her into a floating hotel in a Highland loch came to nothing and, after being sold for a mere £75, she moved to Bo'ness for breaking up. Her replacement for the next six seasons on the 'Mainland run' was even older, having been built in 1871, but her boilers were in a better state of repair. The Aberdeen-London steamer *City of London* duly appeared for the 1931 season as *Lochbroom*. She had sleeping berths for over 80 passengers.

The last of the batch of four new ships was to be "assigned to such service and shall be of such power and capacity as may be agreed between the parties". A truly revolutionary ship was the result, the *Lochfyne* being 'the first British passenger vessel to have the propellers driven by direct-coupled electric motors which received their energy from generators deriving their power from Diesel engines', that is, she was Britain's first diesel electric ship. One disadvantage was the excessive vibration and noise caused by the engines but it was reckoned that this was balanced by the fact that she was very economical to run. Her rôle was to replace the inadequate *Fusilier* on the Staffa and Iona station in summer and the Ardrishaig mail run in winter, which she did admirably. The old paddler left Oban for the first time in her long career and took over the mantle of the ancient *Glencoe* as Portree mail steamer. The veteran of 85 years sailed round to the Clyde and berthed alongside the newcomer at Glasgow Broomielaw as part of Civic and Empire Week, providing a most striking contrast and provoking a huge public interest. She was then scrapped at Ardrossan.

The launch of the *Lochearn* at Ardrossan Dockyard (owned by Coast Lines) in April 1930

Oban North Pier in August 1933 with (left to right) P.S. *Mountainer*, P.S. *Iona* and M.V. *Lochmor*

Graham E Langmuir

1930 saw the last of one of the great favourites of all time in the West Highlands, S.S. *Claymore*; she is seen here alongside Gairloch Pier in Wester Ross

The Aberdeen-London steamer *City of London* appeared for the 1931 season as the replacement for the *Claymore*; the *Lochbroom* is seen here on the River Clyde passing Partick

The cover of the leaflet advertising the *Lochbroom*'s cruises in 1931; it features a hand stamp from Coast Lines Ltd of London

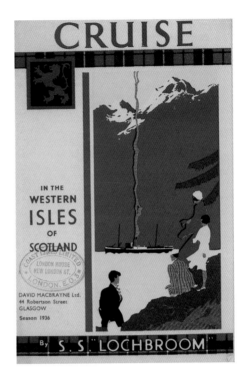

Old and new at Portree - the 83 year old *Glencoe* berthed alongside her replacement, the *Fusilier* of 1888 in May 1931

68

The veteran *Glencoe* berthed alongside the newcomer *Lochfyne* at the Broomielaw, Glasgow, in June 1931

Old and new excursion steamers at Oban's South Pier - P.S. *Mountaineer* alongside D.E.V. *Lochfyne*

New Twin-Screw Vessel, "Lochfyne"

On Oban and Staffa and Iona service during Summer—Greenock and Ardrishaig during Winter

Now that tourists to the Inner and Outer Hebrides have been supplied with unrivalled facilities in the way of magnificent new saloon steamers, the attention of MacBrayne's has been concentrated in a sense on supplying the perfection of comfort for increasing multitudes of people from all over the world who, whatever else they miss of the unrivalled glories of Scotland, seize the opportunity of living crowded hours of glorious and intense life on the unique day's sail from Oban to Staffa and Iona.

Nothing has been spared in the equipment of the new vessel "Lochfyne" towards ensuring the maximum of absolute ease, and the result has been the most up-to-date pleasure steamer in Scotland. The furnishings are luxurious in the artistically designed smoke-rooms and dining-rooms. On the promenade deck there is an Observation Lounge with large windows along the sides, and suitably nearby are a Soda Fountain and Ice-cream Freezer. The vessel is heated throughout by means of a hot water installation. There can be no doubt that the "Lochfyne" will soon establish itself in popularity with tourists to the "Sacred Island."

How the new Lochfyne was sold to the public

The romantic cover of MacBrayne's 1932 timetable

Three years later MacBrayne's Oban fleet received a minor boost when the *Princess Louise* joined them. This 1898 screw steamer of under 100 feet had spent her life offering short cruises out of Oban for one Alexander Paterson or his son. She continued in her usual employment for one further year but between 1935 and 1938 she offered cruises out of Inverness to supplement the sailings of the *Gondolier*.

Meanwhile the *Lochfyne* had proved to be such a winner that a second similar vessel was ordered in time to take up the Portree-Kyle-Mallaig mail run in July 1934 and allow the *Fusilier* to be sold out of the fleet. Smaller and with only one funnel, the *Lochnevis* had one great advantage, namely that the vibration associated with her form of propulsion had been miraculously all but cured. Not long after she took up service one of the main piers in Skye closed amid a fair public outcry. Broadford Pier was in a dilapidated state and had become unsafe. It was to be the first of many traditional piers to shut its gates. Meanwhile MacBraynes' started to buy up several strategic piers like Tobermory, Tarbert (Harris) and Port Ellen. From January 1935 they also leased from the LMS Railway the operation of the short crossing from Kyle of Lochalsh to Kyleakin in Skye, the railway company having just obtained the ferry rights from the original lessee. A new boat, actually owned by the LMS, was soon placed on the crossing. It was capable of transporting two vehicles and incorporated a turntable device to assist loading cars at all states of the tide - again shades of things to come.

Withdrawal of Two Grand Old Ladies

The depression of the early thirties had a positive effect on MacBrayne revenues. Vacations had to be taken at home and English holidaymakers began to seek out Scotland in increasing numbers. Previously the season had peaked during the Glasgow Fair holidays in the second half of July but now August too was becoming increasingly busy. In this atmosphere the LMS from 1933 became involved in negotiations over the assets and goodwill of Williamson-Buchanan Steamers Ltd and Turbine Steamers Ltd, fleets of white-funnelled steamers sailing from Glasgow 'doon the watter' and on the long-haul day excursions to Campbeltown and Inveraray. Eventually on 3 October 1935 David MacBrayne Ltd - the date had now been dropped from the Company's title - obtained the two vessels belonging to Turbine Steamers Ltd, the *Queen Alexandra* and *King George V*, the successors of the steamers which had caused David MacBrayne and his sons so much anguish at the turn of the century.

This allowed the Company to carry out the unthinkable - to withdraw the grand old ladies of the fleet, the *Columba* and *Iona*, the latter by now over 70 years old. At the end of the 1935 season they were laid up in Greenock and early in the following year, amid much public sadness, they were towed to Dalmuir for breaking up. MacBrayne's used considerable initiative to ensure that the Royal Route on the Clyde retained its pre-eminence. The upper deck of the turbine steamer *Queen Alexandra* was extended aft, the funnels were of course painted red and black and a third (dummy) funnel and second mast added. With a stroke of genius the Company renamed the ship *Saint Columba* and as such she took her place on the summer 7.11 a.m. run from Glasgow to Tarbert and Ardrishaig. Her début in 1936 was successful

The *Lochfyne* had proved such a winner that a second similar vessel was ordered to take up the Portree-Kyle-Mallaig mail run in July 1934; the *Lochnevis* is seen here at Gairloch

An atmospheric shot of holidaymakers in Dunoon watching the great *Columba* arrive on her way back from Ardrishaig about four in the afternoon

A deck shot of the *Iona* in her last days of service

In 1935 MacBrayne's were able to carry out the unthinkable - to withdraw the grand old ladies of the fleet, the *Columba* and *Iona*; this forlorn picture shows the two ships laid up in Greenock's East India Harbour awaiting their end

MacBrayne's bought T.S. *Queen Alexandra* and immediately painted her two funnels red as she lay in Greenock's Albert Harbour

MacBrayne's added a third (dummy) funnel and a second mast to the *Queen Alexandra*, renamed her *Saint Columba* and in 1936 placed her on the *Columba*'s run from Glasgow to Ardrishaig

and her performance enhanced a year later when she was converted to burn oil fuel, like the *Lochness*. Meanwhile the *King George V*, with few alterations apart from her funnel colouring, was sent round to Oban for the Staffa and Iona excursion and became instantly popular, despite the high price charged for the day trip. The *Lochfyne* was displaced and took up the *Iona's* Fort William sailings.

Clyde Cargo
The other agreement reached in October 1935 was that David MacBrayne Ltd obtained a controlling interest in Clyde Cargo Steamers Ltd, formed back in the dark days of the Great War to coordinate the various vessels transporting cargo and livestock to all the corners of the Firth.. The company now had three screw ships, the *Ardyne*, *Arran* and *Minard*. In March 1937 the fleet was expanded when the Campbeltown Steam Packet Company's two passenger and cargo vessels *Davaar* and *Dalriada* were acquired. The firm now changed its name to Clyde & Campbeltown Shipping Co Ltd and MacBrayne's funnel colourings were adopted. The passenger service to Campbeltown was grossly uneconomic and MacBrayne's tried unsuccessfully to persuade another LMS subsidiary, The Caledonian Steam Packet Co Ltd, to take over the responsiblilty for it as they already provided fast turbine sailings in summer. In the summer of 1939 the Company failed to have the mail contract renewed and in July they decided finally to withdraw passenger facilities.

More Fleet Replacement
The remaining years of the thirties saw a minor fleet replacement programme, though not necessarily with new tonnage. Thanks to the association with Coast Lines Ltd, MacBrayne's were able to obtain two older vessels from the Burns & Laird Irish fleet. The traditional cargo boat *Lairdspool*, originally the *Lily* of 1896, was transferred, duly overhauled, renamed *Lochgorm* and in February 1937 placed on the Glasgow-Stornoway route in lieu of the *Lochdunvegan*. The latter then became spare and relief vessel and the *Lochiel* was sold for further service. The other ship to be replaced was the *Lochbroom*, which was scrapped after only a few years' service with the Company, and a very fine ship joined the fleet in lieu. Launched as *Vulture* in 1898 and subsequently renamed *Lairdsrock*, she was lying redundant in Ardrossan and had in fact been chartered by MacBrayne's for relief work. Her new Company took her in hand, completely refurbished her internally to a very high standard and gave her a large, imposing oval funnel. As *Lochgarry*, she took her place with pride on the summer ten day mainland cruise, carrying cargo also to the outlying villages in the north west.

The remaining paddle steamers in the fleet were also nearing the end of their useful lives. The *Mountaineer* especially required urgent reboilering after the 1937 season and as this was considered too expensive she was withdrawn. The old *Plover*, relegated to spare steamer on the appearance of the *Lochmor* in 1930, had been renovated in 1934 and had re-emerged as a directors' yacht under the name *Loch Aline*, although she still carried out much relief work in the off season. She now took on the mantle of the Oban short cruise steamer while a small motor launch renamed *Lochbuie* was purchased from Holland and placed on brief forenoon, afternoon and evening cruises from Fort William.

The *King George V* was sent round to Oban in 1935 for the Staffa and Iona excursion to replace the *Lochfyne*; it is believed that this photograph was taken at Iona when this took place, the *King George V* (right) having come from Oban and the *Lochfyne* from Fort William direct

In October 1935 David MacBrayne Ltd obtained a controlling interest in Clyde Cargo Steamers Ltd; the company had three screw ships. The *Ardyne* is seen at Keppel Pier, Cumbrae

76

The Campbeltown SP Company's cargo and passenger steamer *Davaar* berthing at Campbeltown newly sporting MacBrayne funnel colours

The traditional cargo boat *Lairdspool* was renamed *Lochgorm* and placed on the Glasgow-Stornoway route in 1937; here she is seen in Stornoway Harbour

The *Lochgarry* took her place with pride on the summer ten day mainland cruise, carrying cargo also to the outlying villages in the north west

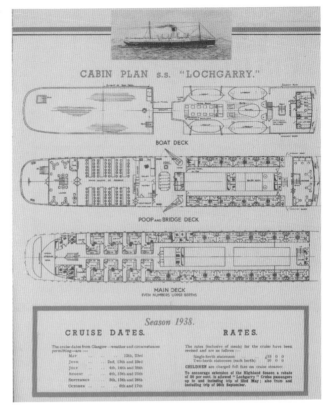

CABIN PLAN s.s. "LOCHGARRY."

BOAT DECK

POOP AND BRIDGE DECK

MAIN DECK
EVEN NUMBERS UPPER BERTHS

A new *Lochiel* was intended to be the *Pioneer*'s replacement on the Islay mail run but West Loch Tarbert pier required a considerable amount of dredging; she is seen here in her first season leaving Oban for Fort William

Season 1938.

CRUISE DATES.   RATES.

A new *Lochiel*, built as a requirement of a new mail contract, was intended to be the *Pioneer's* replacement on the mail run to and from Islay, Jura and Gigha. Not unlike the *Lochnevis* but with her funnel farther aft and her Diesel engines driving twin screws through normal reduction gearing rather than by electrical transmission, she was duly commissioned in the summer. West Loch Tarbert pier, however, proved unsuitable for her because of its shallow approaches: a considerable amount of dredging was required. The *Pioneer* had gone to Oban as a replacement for the *Loch Aline* and it was easy for the two ships merely to exchange places. This was in fact fortuitous as the *Lochfyne* suffered a serious breakdown in late July and the new ship was available to take over the Fort William sailings.

The Second World War
In marked contrast to 1914, the Declaration of War against Germany on 3 September 1939 had an immediate effect on the Clyde and West Highland sailings. Naval grey was donned almost immediately by all units. The Government contract with David MacBrayne Ltd was suspended and all operations controlled by the Ministry of War Transport with several vessels requisitioned to serve under the white ensign. First to go, very briefly, was the *Comet*, but she was returned and remained on station throughout the war years. Next came the *Lochbuie*, which became a hospital launch, and then the *Loch Aline*, berthed at Rothesay as an examination vessel. The veteran Loch Ness paddler *Gondolier* was towed to Orkney and her hull sunk as part of the barrage blocking one of the entrances to Scapa Flow.

The *King George V* distinguished herself in 1940 as a troopship in the English Channel and, after almost being lost following a bomber attack off Boulogne, gave yeoman service during the evacuation of Dunkirk, so much so that her Master, Chief Engineer and Bo'sun were decorated. The excitement over, she spent the rest of the war as a troop tender on the Clyde. The *Lochgarry* was requisitioned too: she survived Dunkirk but in January 1942 sank with the loss of 23 lives after striking rocks off Rathlin Island, in County Antrim, in a severe blizzard.

The *Saint Columba* gave the last ever 0711 sailing from Glasgow on 4 September 1939; with the closure once again of the Cloch-Dunoon boom she was transferred to Wemyss Bay before being laid up from November in Greenock's East India Harbour as an accommodation ship. A further boom across the Kylerhea Narrows between Skye and the mainland also cut off Mallaig and Kyle from each other: the Portree Mail Service was soon suspended and the *Lochnevis* transferred to the white ensign as a minelayer. Finally the Company's last paddle steamer *Pioneer*, having been used a a relief ship to Mull and employed extensively on livestock sailings, was taken over by the Admiralty early in 1944 and anchored off Fairlie on the Clyde as Headquarters for the Submarine Control of the North Atlantic.

Essential services in the Clyde and West Highlands were cut to an absolute minimum during the six years' conflict. The *Lochfyne*, duly repaired, took her place on the Wemyss Bay-Ardrishaig mail run and the Comet was returned to Lochgoilhead. The *Lochinvar* continued to serve Mull, the *Lochearn* the Inner Isles, the *Lochmor* the Outer Isles and the *Lochness* Stornoway. With the West Loch Pier

A wartime shot of the *Lochnevis* approaching Wemyss Bay as she relieved on the Ardrishaig mail run before being transferred to the white ensign as a minelayer *Leo Vogt*

The *King George V* gave yeoman service during the evacuation of Dunkirk but spent the rest of the war as a troop tender on the Clyde; she is seen here berthed at Gourock with the *Duchess of Hamilton* alongside in 1945

suitably dredged, the *Lochiel* was able to take over the Islay run from June 1940. Because of the Kylerhea Boom, the *Lochmor* was based solely at Mallaig and changes to her roster brought to an end passenger calls at Dunvegan in the West of Skye, a port which had been such an important part in David MacBrayne's original services to the Outer Isles. A corollary of the withdrawal of the Portree mail run was the increase in traffic using the short crossing from Kyle to Kyleakin. Another turntable ferry, the first built of steel rather than wood, was added in 1942.

An interesting development took place during the war when MacBrayne's started operating buses for the first time away from the mainland. The services of Neil McGibbon of Bowmore on Islay were acquired in 1941.

Although there were very few holidaymakers travelling, traffic kept up because of troop movements and there were fewer peaks than in peacetime. Tiree, for example, was an important RAF base during the war and the *Lochearn*, with her limited capacity, could not cope on her own. From 1941 MacBrayne's were allowed to charter the *Hebrides* (1898) from their friendly rivals Messrs McCallum Orme, a concern which had for many years employed a small number of cargo and passenger vessels on weekly sailings round the islands from Glasgow. The *Lochearn* normally concentrated on Barra and Lochboisdale while the older ship served Coll and Tiree. As a *quid pro quo* MacBrayne's leased the *Lochgorm* to McCallum Orme.

At the outbreak of war there were four MacBrayne cargo vessels working out of Glasgow. The *Lochshiel* continued on the Kinlochleven run while the *Lochdunvegan* took over the Islay service from 1940. The only other vessel remaining to cover the Stornoway and Mainland services was the *Clydesdale* and, as she was required for extended periods to cover the mailboats' annual refits, extensive chartering resulted. One vessel, the *Ulster Star*, was on constant charter from 1942, so much so that on the cessation of hostilities she was repainted in MacBrayne colours.

Despite the dangers from enemy submarines and mines no serious accident occurred throughout the six long years. The public stoically put up with relief vessels distinctly below the normal acceptable standards, over-crowding, blackouts, late running and diversions until at last, on 8 May 1945, the War in Europe ceased. It took some time before a semblance of normality returned, although the *Lochnevis*, relief vessel since leaving the Admiralty's service in 1944, did manage some cruises out of Oban during the 1945 summer. The symptoms which were in evidence after the First World War were repeated after the Second, except that strike threats had diminished but the dangers of inflation were much more manifest. Costs and wages kept on rising but fares did not show a corresponding increase. The *Loch Aline* and the *Lochbuie* were not recommissioned after the War, the *Pioneer* remained under Admiralty control and of course the *Gondolier* and *Lochgarry* had been lost. In addition the *Saint Columba* was not available for service until 1947.

Post-War Retrenchment

In 1946 the *King George V* remained on the Clyde as Ardrishaig mail steamer throughout the season, but from Gourock rather than Glasgow and Greenock. The year also turned out to be the last for the *Comet* on the Lochgoilhead service as the Company decided that they could not thole such a drain on their limited resources: the little motor ship was withdrawn in October amid much public protest and one of the oldest steamboat routes in the world was brought to a close. The *Lochiel* was now thirled to the Islay route and, with the *Hebrides* back under the flag of McCallum Orme, the *Lochearn* had to cope with the diminished traffic on the Tiree-Barra run herself. The *Lochinvar* remained as the Sound of Mull mailboat, but the Oban excursions were somewhat decimated, as only the *Lochfyne* was available to cover both Staffa and Iona and Fort William. In the event the Company chartered a smallish, old-fashioned but quite attractive steamer from Coast Lines, the *Robina*, to supplement her sailings with short cruises. Farther north, the *Lochmor* was able once again to use Kyle as her base, the *Lochnevis* had returned to Portree the previous November, although, thanks to the increased popularity of the short crossing to Kyleakin, her popularity had waned, and the *Lochness* soldiered on at Stornoway. The Kyle-Kyleakin ferry service, incidentally, had been taken into the LMS Railway's own control on 1 January 1945 on the expiry of MacBrayne's lease. Not surprisingly, sailings on Loch Ness were never resumed. Although the cargo fleet was at full strength the *Clydesdale* was still being used frequently for general and relief work and the *Ulster Star* was kept on to assist, especially on the mainland service. The regular fleet, then, was down to thirteen major vessels plus the *Saint Columba* laid up and two vessels on charter.

The following year the *Saint Columba* at last returned to peacetime service and the *King George V* could resume her place at Oban. The *Robina* was no longer required. As a sop to the villagers of Lochgoilhead, however, the Company bowed to pressure and she provided a seasonal service in succession to the *Comet* under an extension to her charter. The financial results were dismal and the route was never reopened. Another vessel did appear at Oban that year: as a result of yet another mail contract, MacBraynes' purchased a hospital launch which had been working on the Clyde, renamed her *Lochnell* and placed her on a new service to the island of Lismore at the end of June.

A New Mailboat

The main event of 1947, however, was the commissioning of a fine new ship for the Stornoway mail service. The mail contract of 1938 had specified a new vessel not just for Islay but also for Stornoway. While the *Lochiel* duly appeared, war delayed the ordering of a *Lochness* replacement until 1945 and then, because of the acute shortage of materials, the launch of the *Loch Seaforth* was impossible before May 1947 and her commissioning was put back until December. The latest addition to the fleet was the largest ever built for Stornoway; her 14 knot speed together with her superior accommodation and fittings immediately endeared her to the Lewis islanders and she became an instant success. She was, incidentally, the first member of the fleet to be equipped with radar. The old *Lochness* saw out the next few years as spare vessel, spending a considerable time on the Inner Islands mail run to allow

Gourock in 1946 showing the *King George V* at the head of the pier loading for Tarbert and Ardrishaig and a war-weary *Duchess of Montrose* setting off for Arran   James Simpson

After the war the *Lochmor* was able once again to use Kyle of Lochalsh as her base, as in this photograph

The *Saint Columba* arriving at Lamont's slip, Port Glasgow, for reconditioning after the War - she was the last ship in Britain to be released from Admiralty service; in the background is the stern of the *King George V*, being made ready for her first post-war season back in Oban

Captain Bob McLean of the *Saint Columba*

As a sop to the villagers of Lochgoilhead the chartered *Robina* provided a seasonal service from Gourock; she is seen here in her overnight berth along with the *Saint Columba* at Greenock's Customhouse Quay

At the time the largest vessel ever built for Stornoway; the *Loch Seaforth* is seen here loading at Kyle of Lochalsh in June 1950

Graham E Langmuir

85

the *Lochearn, Lochmor* and *Lochinvar* to be re-engined in turn in an attempt to increase their speed. This was a winning strategy as all three motor vessels were given a new lease of life and their reputations greatly enhanced.

Takeover

1 January 1948 was a date of great significance for David MacBrayne Ltd. Not only were the shares owned by the LMS nationalised and transferred to the British Transport Commission ("British Railways") under the Labour Government's Transport Act of 1947, but the Company also acquired the ships and goodwill of McCallum, Orme & Co Ltd. The latter appeared at the time to have greater significance in the eyes of the public. Now for the first time MacBrayne's were responsible for cargo sailings from Glasgow to Colonsay, Iona, Coll, Tiree, the Uists, Harris and the West of Skye. The McCallum Orme steamers had a long pedigree and had been providing services to the Western Isles in one form or another for nearly a hundred years. Unlike the MacBrayne empire which expanded west from the Royal Route, the rival ships had from the start concentrated on providing a service to the islands themselves. The workings of the two companies had been complementary to each other and the relationships between them friendly and positive. Three vessels were purchased. While the *Hebrides* was welcomed back as a familiar friend thanks to her wartime charter, the other two ships, the once-renowned *Dunara Castle* and the cargo boat *Challenger*, had reached the end of their useful service and were soon scrapped.

One additional burden on MacBrayne's was to provide passenger as well as cargo sailings to Colonsay, as no mailboat had normally touched at the island. At the time of the amalgamation the *Lochness* happened to be on the Inner Islands run from Oban. Colonsay was immediately added as a port of call but in the summer she made a special trip there from Oban, giving a fine excursion sailing in the process. From 1949, however, the Colonsay call was added to the roster of the Islay mailboat and the *Lochiel* extended her sailing on Port Askaig days, returning to spend the night at the Islay port.

Cargo Ship Retrenchment

MacBrayne's own cargo vessels had themselves seen a great deal of service and it is not surprising that the restructured company made its main priority for the following few years the modernisation and streamlining of this sector of their business and the rationalisation of the rosters of the two cargo fleets. The *Lochdunvegan* was the first to be withdrawn, in April 1948. She was replaced on the Glasgow-Islay route first by the *Clydesdale* and then more permanently by a new motor vessel built at the end of the war as a coastal patrol ship, the *Empire Maysong*. Converted from steam to diesel, fitted out for her new occupation at Ardrossan and renamed *Lochbroom*, she took over the service in the summer of that year. Gradually the MacBrayne and McCallum Orme calls were integrated and motor transport substituted for many of the satellite ports of call, so that by the end of 1948 the number of cargo vessels in the combined fleet was down by two. MacBrayne's too gradually absorbed many small independent bus operators on the islands so that the Company's buses could be found on Mull, Skye, Harris and the Uists.

In 1948 David MacBrayne Ltd acquired the ships and goodwill of McCallum, Orme & Co Ltd. The poster indicates the six cargo services offered in February 1948 before the rosters of the two companies were properly integrated

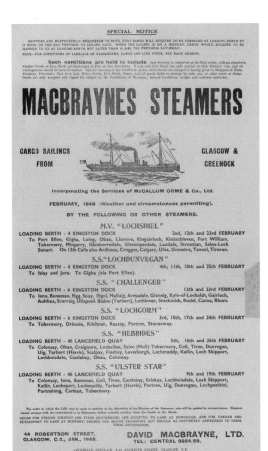

The *Hebrides* of 1898 was welcomed back to MacBrayne's thanks to a wartime charter; she is seen here in June 1948 off Bowling on the Clyde

Graham E Langmuir

87

The old and the new in Kingston Dock, Glasgow; the *Lochdunvegan* (left) and *Hebrides* in April 1952

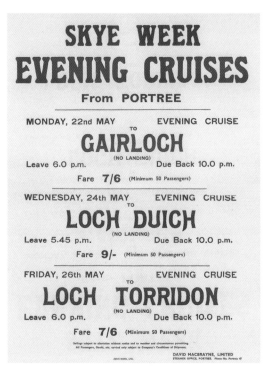

A poster advertising the evening cruises of the *Lochnevis* from Portree during Skye Week 1950

1949 saw further judicious pruning, although an additional small vessel entered the fleet. In terms of the 1947 mail contract a new service was to be operated between Tobermory and Mingary in Ardnamurchan, partly as the Mull capital was as the crow flies the nearest shopping centre to the outlying community and partly to save the Outer Isles mailboat having to call as connection could conveniently be made at Tobermory. The boat purchased was a former RAF rescue pinnace which was extensively refitted and renamed *Lochbuie*.

It was at this time that Mr H T Leith, the General Manager of the Company for the previous 23 years, retired, being replaced by Mr H S McLauchlan, formerly manager in Oban. A year later it was the turn of Sir Alfred Read, Chairman since the Company's reorganisation in 1928, to intimate his retirement. He was succeeded by Mr I P R Napier.

The long-term charter of the *Ulster Star* was terminated when MacBrayne's bought a Dutch cargo ship *Marleen*, similar to the *Empire Maysong*. Unlike her she was not converted to diesel and so became the last ever steam vessel to be commissioned by the Company. Her name was changed to *Loch Frisa* and from June 1949 she partnered the *Hebrides* on what was known as the Outer Isles cargo run, plying to the same ports and alternating with her more senior consort. The *Lochgorm* was next to be withdrawn, in December 1950, when her replacement entered service. This was a new *Lochdunvegan*, formerly the *Örnen* from Sweden, and she became closely identified with the Stornoway route.

Centenary
The centenary of Hutcheson/MacBrayne was celebrated on 10 February 1951 when eighteen MacBrayne vessels in sea or in harbour were dressed overall. The following table, when the details are compared with those of 1901, shows the changes, modernisation and diminution of the fleet, but essentially the services, especially those of the mail steamers, had not changed very significantly.

ROUTE	VESSEL
Gourock-Ardrishaig	*T.S. Saint Columba*
Islay-West Loch Tarbert	*M.V. Lochiel*
Tobermory-Oban	*M.V. Lochinvar*
Tobermory-Mingary	*M.V. Lochbuie*
Oban-Tiree-Barra	*M.V. Lochearn*
Oban-Staffa-Iona	*T.S. King Geroge V*
Oban-Fort William, etc.	*D.E.V. Lochfyne*
Oban-Lismore	*M.V. Lochnell*
Kyle-Mallaig-Outer Isles	*M.V. Lochmor*
Portree-Kyle-Mallaig	*D.E.V. Lochnevis*
Stornoway-Kyle-Mallaig	*M.V. Loch Seaforth*
Glasgow-Islay	*M.V. Lochbroom*
Glasgow-Kinlochleven	*M.V. Lochshiel*
Glasgow-Outer Isles	*S.S. Hebrides*
Glasgow-Outer Isles	*S.S. Loch Frisa*

The centenary of Hutcheson/MacBrayne was celebrated on 10 February 1951; a brochure was published by the Company to commemorate the event

The cover of MacBrayne's Centenary Year summer timetable, 1951

Glasgow-Stornoway	*M.V. Lochdunvegan*
Glasgow-North Mainland	*S.S. Clydesdale*
Spare vessel	*S.S. Lochness*
Laid up	*S.S. Lochgorm*

The number of buses in the fleet had meantime risen from one to 112, the daily mileage from 42 to 7200 and the route mileage from 21 to 1182.

Mail Contract Obligations

Yet another mail contract, dating from 1949, had specified that a new ship be built for the Outer Isles cargo service; this had the added advantage that the almost new steamship *Loch Frisa*, when displaced, could act as a general cargo and livestock carrier and as a relief ship. Ardrossan Dockyard was given the contract and the *Loch Carron*, a larger development of the *Lochbroom*, duly appeared in service in April 1951. Four months later it was decided that all cargo for the mainland communities north of Kyle of Lochalsh was to be transported by lorry. MacBrayne's cleverly dovetailed the *Clydesdale's* Mainland cargo run with the *Lochshiel's* service to Mull, Loch Sunart and Loch Leven and the latter ship was sold. The combined roster became known as the Inner Isles cargo run. Within two years, however, the Company further rationalised their cargo services and this amalgamated schedule ceased altogether, some calls being transferred to the Outer Isles ships and some made instead by road transport. It was time, amid general regret, for the *Clydesdale* to be withdrawn from the fleet. MacBrayne's last "*-dale*" had probably made more calls and sailed on more routes than any of their other ships, in peace or war. In the seven years since the end of the war the number of cargo boats left in the combined MacBrayne/McCallum Orme fleet had been reduced to four, wth one spare, and well over twenty ports of call had been axed.

That same year, 1953, the Company were asked to take over the operation of the service in Loch Shiel, running from Glenfinnan on the West Highland Railway to Acharacle in Ardnamurchan. This they duly did and placed two launches on the loch, the *Rosalind*, renamed *Lochshiel*, and the *Lochailort*. The service lasted until the building of an important road which opened up the area in 1967.

By now only three vessels built before the Great War - the *Hebrides*, *Lochinvar* and *Saint Columba* - remained in the fleet and the minor changes which took place over the next ten years or so were designed to replace them. David MacBrayne Ltd signed a mail contract in 1952 which gave them a fairly substantial subsidy and which stipulated that two new vessels had to be commissioned. Both entered the fleet in 1955.

First came the *Claymore*, an imposing, modern-looking ship which quite outclassed in size, speed and accommodation the *Lochearn* she replaced. This of course was on the thrice weekly voyage from Oban to Tobermory, Coll, Tiree, Barra and Lochboisdale, known locally as the "Barra'boisdale run". Incidentally she was the first ship since the restructuring of 1928 to break the "Loch" rule in nomenclature. The *Lochness* was sold to the Greeks and the *Lochearn* became the Mull mail boat,

The 1949 mail contract specified that a new ship be built for the Outer Isles cargo service; this was the *Loch Carron* which appeared in service in 1951; she is seen here at Castlebay, Barra

An evocative photograph of the *King George V* in Lamont's drydock, Greenock, in 1953, with the *Lochiel* in the East India Harbour behind

although she was used for reliefs in winter. The old *Lochinvar* in turn became spare, but was to be found on her 'own run' frequently in winter when the *Lochearn* was elsewhere. The *Claymore* found additional employment giving short trips from Oban, one being of considerable significance. Already on the Clyde The Caledonian Steam Packet Company had very successfully introduced three hoist-loading vehicle ferries to cope with the huge increase in car travel since petrol had been derationed. MacBrayne's interim response, in the absence of any funds to follow suit, was where possible to provide special sailings specifically for cars. For this reason the *Claymore* sailed on Saturday afternoons from Oban to Salen, the nearest suitable pier on Mull, but as she still loaded by derrick, in a sense she was obsolete as soon as she entered the water.

The second ship was MacBrayne's last cargo boat, the *Loch Ard*, easily distinguished from her consorts by her self-supporting bipod mast with derricks fore and aft, giving her the distinction of being able to lift 10 tons, the heaviest load of any vessel in the fleet. She now took over from the former MacCallum Orme flagship *Hebrides* as the *Loch Carron's* partner on the Outer Isles cargo run, the old favourite being sold for scrap.

No further significant changes occurred until the 1959 season, although a small vessel was commissioned in 1956. Just as the *Lochbuie*, by providing sailings to and from Mingary, saved the Outer Isles mailboat from calling there, so the appearance of the *Loch Toscaig* - the former motor fishing vessel *Irene Julia* - on a new route between Kyle of Lochalsh and Toscaig, on the Applecross peninsula, obviated the need for the Stornoway mail steamer to make her traditional ferry call at Applecross, likewise saving a fair amount of time.

Skye Problems

MacBrayne's scheme announced in the summer of 1958 was to withdraw the remaining two pre-Great War veterans and put an end to the grossly uneconomic Portree mail service. With the increase in motor vehicles almost all traffic to Skye now went via the CSP's car ferry service between Kyle and Kyleakin and new and more substantial turntable ferries had been periodically added to the route. The people of Skye were not happy and a compromise had to be reached. In 1959 the *Lochnevis* was indeed withdrawn as the Portree mailboat and transferred to Oban for the excursions to Fort William, etc. This allowed the *Lochfyne* to remain as Ardrishaig mail steamer throughout the year and not just in winter. The ultimate reason for carrying out these changes was to save recommissioning the *Saint Columba*, that unique three-funnelled turbine which had graced the waters of the Clyde for so long and which, sadly, was badly in need of boiler repairs. She had given her last voyage on 27 September 1958.

The compromise was that the old *Lochinvar*, spare since 1955, was sent to Skye to take the *Lochnevis*'s place as in the eyes of the public the time was not ripe to withdraw the mail service completely. The *Lochinvar* was a disaster in her new rôle and she did not survive past the end of October. By early in the following year she had been sold. Bowing to public opinion, MacBrayne's had sought a new ship to

The imposing, modern-looking ship *Claymore* was commissioned on the thrice weekly voyage from Oban to Coll, Tiree, Barra and Lochboisdale in 1955; she is seen here taking cars to Salen, Mull, in August 1957
J Aikman Smith

The *Lochearn* of 1930 displaced by the new *Claymore* to the Sound of Mull route: here she is seen with the tender alongside at Craignure in 1961
Graham E Langmuir

MacBrayne's last cargo boat, the *Loch Ard,* became the *Loch Carron*'s partner on the Outer Isles cargo run in 1955; later she was transferred to Islay and she is seen here at the distillery pier at Bunnahabhain in June 1968
W M Russell

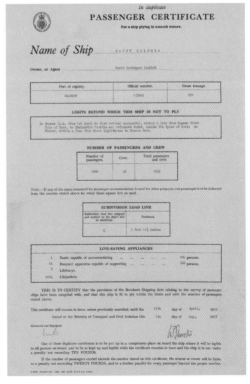

The Class V Passenger certificate of the Saint Columba valid from May 1957 till April 1958

The *Saint Columba* had graced the waters of the Clyde for many years but in 1958 was badly in need of boiler repairs and had to be withdrawn; this fine shot was taken on her first day in service after the War

The former Mull steamer *Lochinvar* was a disaster in her 1959 rôle as Portree mail boat; she is seen here leaving Kyle of Lochalsh in July *Edwin J Wylie*

fulfil their obligations and so purchased a wooden inshore minesweeper which was stripped, given a new lightweight aluminium superstructure and renamed *Loch Arkaig*. She took up the service on a more permanent basis in April 1960, the *Lochearn* and *Lochnevis* having filled in meantime.

The Coming of the Car Ferry

Mr C B Leith, son of the long-serving General Manager H T Leith, had taken over his father's position in 1959. It was he who announced at the commissioning of the *Loch Arkaig* in 1960 the far reaching plans to commission dual-purpose vessels to the Western Isles. Three new car ferries were to be introduced as soon as possible, most likely to sail between Mallaig and Armadale, between the North of Skye, North Uist and Harris and between Oban, Mull and Morvern. Thanks to the construction of causeways, one of which had just been completed, there was now a road running right from North Uist through Benbecula to South Uist so that Lochmaddy could serve the whole of that part of the Outer Isles. Skye, with its much-improved road system, could justifiably be used as a link between the mainland and the Outer Isles, thus permitting a short sea crossing. At the same time all remaining cargo services to Skye's western seaboard could be withdrawn. This happened in July 1962 when the two Outer Isles cargo services were telescoped into one with the axeing of a further nine calls. The *Loch Ard* was transferred to Islay, the *Lochbroom* relegated to spare vessel and the *Loch Frisa* sold to the Greeks.

The problem was that to finance MacBrayne's ambitious plans required more than the normal annual subsidy of £300,000. In 1960 the Government passed the Highlands and Islands Shipping Services Act by which the Secretary of State for Scotland was to be empowered to build and charter ships. A new Government contract for ten years announced in December 1961 stated explicitly that in order to finance the proposed new car ferries the 1960 Act would be invoked, in other words the Secretary of State would order the ships and then charter them to David MacBrayne Ltd. They would be registered at Leith. It took a further year before the orders were actually placed - with Hall, Russell of Aberdeen after intense competition. Meanwhile ancillary works were proceeding apace to ensure that the service could actually start on time. Terminals were confirmed as Uig in North Skye, which required major renovation, and, less controversially, Lochmaddy in North Uist and Tarbert in Harris. Lochaline in Morvern had already been modified but Craignure in Mull had always relied on a ferry call and so a completely new pier was required there: it was completed in December 1963. In addition the Company purchased in late 1961 the pilot boat *Valonia* from the Commissioners of Irish Lights as a possible vessel to serve the Small Isles of Eigg, Muck, Rhum and Canna, historically served by the Outer Isles mailboat, as this facility would obviously be withdrawn.

November 1963 saw the launch of the first of the triplets. Appropriately named *Hebrides* - and with the bell of the famous old "*Heb*" presented to her - the new ship towered above the existing vessels in the fleet. With turntables and four hydraulic rams forward of the passenger accommodation, with space in her car deck or 'garage' for 50 cars and with 50 sleeping berths and a complement of 600 passengers

The *Hebrides* truly started the car ferry revolution when she entered service on 15 April 1964; prior to that she 'showed the flag' at Bridge Wharf,Glasgow. She is seen here canting in the river on 8 April

Graham E Langmuir

MacBrayne's car sticker advertising their new Hebridean Highways in 1964

the *Hebrides* truly started the car ferry revolution when she entered service on 15 April 1964. She was an ideal ship to carry out the dual function of transporting essential vehicles and supplies to and from the islands and at the same time promoting the tourist traffic which was such an important sector of the islands' economy.

The second sister, the *Clansman*, entered service on 5 June on the Mallaig-Armadale crossing, greatly augmented, while the third, the *Columba*, took her place on the newly-cast Oban-Craignure-Lochaline service on 30 July. As had happened on the Clyde ten years before traffic exceeded all expectations and, inevitably, there were delays at peak periods and at low tide, there being a limit as to how fast the ships' hoists could operate. The faithful *Lochmor* was now redundant and, after a period serving Armadale and the Small Isles, was sent to Oban to assist the *Lochearn*, valiantly trying to cope with the new car ferry roster for the two or three months until the *Columba* arrived. Each of the conventional motorships was carrying up to 70 cars per day, which, with loading by the old-fashioned derrick, was no mean feat. Eventually, however, they were able to leave the fray: the twins were withdrawn and sold in August to the Greeks.

The motivation behind the new ships was almost entirely to enhance the provision for tourists and their cars rather than to handle cargo: hence the *Clansman* with a half hour passage time had extensive sleeping accommodation. It was a further thirteen years before the last all-the-way cargo service was to be withdrawn. The remaining three cargo ships actually made a fair profit in 1964, their carryings were increasing and, when the state of the trunk roads to the mainland terminals was taken into account, the most convenient method of handling bulk cargo still seemed to be the time-honoured way of loading by derrick into the hold at Kingston Dock in Glasgow and having it transported directly to its destination.

Meanwhile the little *Valonia* had been commissioned as *Loch Eynort*, but not on the Small Isles service as had originally been intended. Instead she served on the Portree-Raasay-Kyle of Lochalsh station (not extended to Mallaig) and it was the *Loch Arkaig*, complete with a new samson post and derrick for cargo handling, which took up the Small Isles roster. This was eminently sensible as the Portree service was grossly unprofitable, Skye was becoming even more accessible by car as the *Clansman* was supplementing the Kyle ferries with seven crossings per day in summer, and the *Loch Arkaig* had catering facilities, albeit rudimentary, which could be well utilised on her round of the Small Isles combined with an excursion programme from Mallaig. In fact the *Loch Eynort* carried so little traffic in 1964 that next year the *Loch Arkaig* carried out the combined roster and the *Loch Eynort* spent the rest of her days with the Company largely laid up on the Clyde. At the same time Toscaig was served from Kyle by an even smaller and more economical vessel than the *Loch Toscaig*, a motor launch appropriately renamed *Applecross*; she also started a new short-lived service to Kylerhea in Skye as a subsitute for the calls which had been made at Glenelg on the mainland opposite by steamers between Mallaig and Kyle. From 1965 until road transport took over in 1971 MacBrayne's managed both services by chartering them out to a local operator. The other

The third MacBrayne car ferry *Columba* took her place on the newly-cast Oban-Craignure-Lochaline service on 30 July 1964; she is seen at Craignure on that day   *IMcC*

The little *Valonia*, commissioned as *Loch Eynort*, served on the Portree-Raasay-Kyle of Lochalsh in 1964; she is seen here leaving Armadale in May 1970   *J Aikman Smith*

The *Loch Arkaig* took up the Small Isles roster in 1964 on the withdrawal of the *Lochmor*; she is seen here receiving passengers from the *Western Isles* in Loch Scavaig in September of that year

Graham E Langmuir

A redundant ferry from Ballachulish, renamed *Scalpay*, took over the crossing to Scalpay in 1965; she is seen here at Kyles Scalpay in July of that year

Lawrence J Macduff

community left out by the car ferry developments was Scalpay, the island at the mouth of East Loch Tarbert, Harris. It was served by a local fishing boat until a turntable ferry, redundant after a bridge was built at Ballachulish over Loch Leven, took over in May 1965. She was rechristened *Scalpay*: like other MacBrayne small craft her hull was painted red.

The Islay Dilemma

The car ferry revolution had completely bypassed Islay and the other islands in the south and yet vehicle traffic increased there too. In an effort to deal with the situation MacBrayne's in the summer of 1965 transferred the *Lochnevis* from Oban to act as Islay mail steamer while the *Lochiel* assumed the rôle of car carrier. The gap in the Oban excursion programme was partly filled by utilising the *Claymore* in her afternoons free from the Barra'boisdale run. This was, of course, only a stop-gap and the Company came up with proposals in June to place a fully fledged car ferry on the Islay route sailing from a new terminal near the mouth of West Loch Tarbert. The new vessel could also cover Colonsay (now in possession of a pier for the first time), Jura could be served by small ferry from Port Askaig and Gigha likewise from the mainland. The Ardrishaig mail service would be withdrawn as it was not sensible for a passenger only vessel to feed into a car ferry at Tarbert. Calls at Port Ellen in the south end of Islay, and at Craighouse, Jura, would cease. Predictably a war of words arose between the north and south of Islay. A faction arose advocating an "Overland Route" to Islay through Jura: Argyll County Council, while supporting certain aspects of MacBrayne's plan, prevaricated.

As the Islay debate intensified, a private company was formed to provide frequent, cheap services using unsophisticated ships and terminals, combined with low crewing. It was backed by many of the commercial interests in Islay and Jura. It used as an exemplar the type of service prevalent in the Norwegian fjords, an area not dissimilar to the west coast of Scotland, which worked very successfully. Western Ferries Ltd leased land at Kennacraig, near MacBraynes' proposed site, and started to build a basic terminal, as they also did at Port Askaig. As theirs was not to be a subsidised service no consultation exercise was needed. They also ordered a stern-loading ferry from Port Glasgow. This was the *Sound of Islay* and she duly entered service in April 1968. She sailed with a crew of only seven and with vending machines instead of catering but her clientele, car and commerical vehicle drivers, did not mind. She soon ate into MacBrayne's traffic, fairly predictably as motorists naturally preferred to reverse on to a car deck than have their vehicles lifted into the *Lochiel's* cargo hold by crane. So successful was she in fact that Western Ferries ordered another ferry, this time from Norway, which was larger and had superior accommodation - the *Sound of Jura* was the West of Scotland's first drive-through sea-going vessel. Meanwhile a small landing craft was modified for the crossing between Port Askaig and Feolin in the west of Jura: this appeared as the *Sound of Gigha*. Western Ferries soon prospered at the expense of MacBrayne's and the galling aspect for the Company was that the proposals, though on a different scale and excluding Colonsay, were almost exactly their own which had been stillborn thanks to local wrangling.

In the summer of 1965 MacBrayne's transferred the *Lochnevis* to act as Islay mail steamer; she is seen here at Port Ellen in 1969   *J Aikman Smith*

The Lochfyne, being surplus to requirements, was withdrawn in September 1969; she is seen here arriving at Ardrishaig on 16 August of that year   *J Aikman Smith*

1968 saw some action at last. After some three years the Government in February gave their approval to the construction of a terminal at Redhouse, just down from Kennacraig, and they rejected the Overland Route on the grounds of expense for the infrastructure. In December MacBrayne's were able to order their new car ferry from Ailsa, Troon. The Company's jubilation turned quickly sour, however, when Argyll County Council in January 1969 decided not to proceed with the construction of the terminal at Redhouse, giving as their excuse costs and difficulties over land acquisition.

STG
An event of the utmost significance had taken place on 1 January 1969. The Scottish Transport Group (STG) came into being under the 1968 Transport Act. It was set up by the Government as an umbrella under which the dominant Scottish Bus Group, together with the CSP on the Clyde and MacBrayne's in the Western Isles, could operate. The group immediately acquired the 50% holding in David MacBrayne Ltd held by British Railways, and on 1 July they also purchased Coast Lines' half share. For the first time David MacBrayne Ltd was wholly nationalised.

The Scottish Transport Group, under the chairmanship of Mr (later Sir) Patrick Thomas, made an initial appraisal and soon realised that significant changes were needed if a really effective service were to be provided. The number of foot passengers was declining relative to the number travelling in vehicles, while freight companies preferred their cargo carried in lorries without trans-shipping. The number of dual-purpose vessels in the fleet was insufficient to respond to this trend, hoist-loading was slow and restrictive and many of the piers in use had been built with a greatly different form of traffic in mind. The Group wanted to develop "modern roll on-roll off ferry services provided by multi-purpose vessels capable of carrying a mix of cars, coaches and maximum capacity lorries with terminals equipped with end-loading facilities to enable drive through operation". This was a high-sounding mission statement but within a few years a fair amount of it had actually been achieved. So that the MacBrayne management could concentrate on this task the MacBrayne buses were hived off to other Scottish Bus Group Companies, especially Highland Omnibuses. The omnipresent traditional red and green colours were replaced by red and blue. The lorries too were transferred to a newly created Freight Division.

The STG were not slow in making their presence felt in marine matters. The first visible effect was the transfer of the Royal Route from Gourock to Tarbert and Ardrishaig, the latter call now rostered only in summer, to the CSP. The *Lochfyne*, being surplus to requirements, was withdrawn on 30 September 1969, the end of the line for a service which had continued virtually unbroken in peace and in war since 1851 and before. The Caledonian paddle steamer *Caledonia* took over briefly (before she too was withdrawn) and then the service was entrusted to one of the CSP's "Maid" class vessels for eight months, after which it ceased altogether as a mail service. It was at least partly replaced by a car ferry service from Fairlie to Brodick and Tarbert.

Return to Islay

Meanwhile the new Group had had to respond to the Islay question. After searching in vain for a new site for a terminal in West Loch Tarbert, they produced a novel solution to the problem. The new build could be commissioned on the Clyde and give much-needed extra capacity there, say, on the Gourock-Dunoon run, while one of the original CSP car ferries, capable of using the existing terminal in the West Loch, could be transferred to MacBrayne's for the Islay route. It was the pioneer car ferry *Arran* which was duly transferred in November 1969, but she came once again under CSP ownership three months later and afterwards MacBrayne's merely chartered her. Resplendent in full MacBrayne colours and only slightly modified, the *Arran* duly took her place on the traditional Islay service, using her hoist, in January 1970. She soon won a proportion of the traffic back.

The *Lochiel* was now redundant and entered the sale list, as, in October 1969, had the *Lochnevis*. STG, against the wishes of their subsidiary, had insisted that as she was no longer required to relieve at Islay or on the Clyde, her retention merely as a secondary Oban cruise vessel would be an expensive luxury. Her duties as a livestock carrier during the period of the sales could be covered by one of the car ferries, they argued. Fairly obviously, the Islay cargo vessel *Loch Ard* was rendered superfluous on the arrival of the *Arran* and she too was withdrawn. Finally, the argument about retaining the *Lochnevis* was rehearsed also with the spare cargo boat *Lochbroom*. In one short year STG had axed five major units from the MacBrayne fleet and, in so doing, had made the Company much more efficient.

As a *quid pro quo* the *Clansman*, with her funnel painted CSP yellow and black, took up service between Gourock and Dunoon, also in January 1970, the largest and best appointed vessel ever to appear on that particular route. She remained there until the new ship, launched as *Iona*, appeared at the end of May. She also sported a yellow funnel and to all intents and purposes was treated as part of the CSP fleet. As she had to use her hoist to load and unload she frequently found it difficult to keep to time but when end-loading terminals were eventually completed, she came into her own as a drive-through ferry.

That 1970 summer was the first which was quite different from the historical pattern of services. There was no MacBrayne steamer on the Clyde; Islay was served, on a traditional roster, by a car ferry, the *Arran*; there were only three major vessels based at Oban - the *King George V* as the sole excursion steamer, the *Columba* as the Craignure and Lochaline car ferry and the *Claymore* on the Inner Isles run; three vessels served Mallaig - the car ferry *Clansman* for Armadale, the *Loch Arkaig* for the Small Isles, Raasay and Portree and the *Loch Seaforth* for Kyle and Stornoway; while the *Hebrides* was on the 'Uig triangle'. Only two conventional cargo vessels remained, the *Loch Carron* and *Lochdunvegan*, while Lismore, Mingary and Scalpay were served by small vessels. Services on Loch Shiel had ceased. One significant new service was inaugurated the following summer when the *Clansman* on the Mallaig-Armadale station extended her sailings to Barra and Lochboisdale overnight. This removed a great deal of pressure from the *Claymore*, the limited

The *Arran*, resplendent in full MacBrayne colours, took her place on the traditional Islay service in January 1970; here she is seen at Port Ellen making connection with MacBrayne buses for Port Askaig and Portnahaven in September of that year *Graham E Langmuir*

The *Clansman*, with her funnel painted CSP yellow and black, took up service between Gourock and Dunoon in January 1970; here she is on passage on a fine winter's day a month later
Lawrence J Macduff

The new *Iona* sported a yellow funnel and to all intents and purposes was a part of the CSP fleet when she took her place on the Gourock-Dunoon service in 1970; here she is seen leaving Dunoon and passing the statue of Highland Mary that summer *J Aikman Smith*

A fine morning shot of the *King George V* in Oban Bay in the sixties

capacity in her hold being used more for vehicles for Tiree, where there was no alternative service.

The dénouement of the Islay saga was still some way off. Despite the appearance of the *Arran* Western Ferries still had the upper hand and it came as no surprise when the Government announced in November 1971 that the subsidy to MacBrayne's for their service to Islay, Jura, Gigha and Colonsay was to be withdrawn and instead Western Ferries were to be subsidised to extend their operation to Colonsay. The STG had no alternative but to announce that MacBrayne's would withdraw from 31 March 1972 and the *Arran* return to the Clyde. What did come as a surprise was the number of objections lodged against this proposal - 587 in total. The islanders suddenly appeared to realise how much they depended on MacBrayne's. A public enquiry was held where a great deal of acrimonious discussion took place, but in the end MacBrayne's were not permitted to withdraw from Islay and the other southern islands and their subsidy was once again secure. Originally this was to be reviewed at the end of the following September but the arrangement was continued indefinitely; in fact in the autumn of 1972 the STG were negotiating for a takeover of Western Ferries. Although there was considerable opposition to this proposal from the islands the principal shareholders were on the verge of acceptance when a 'white knight', the landowner Sir William Lithgow, through his Dornoch Shipping Co Ltd, made a new bid and this was accepted. The company then became Western Ferries (Argyll) Ltd.

Roll-on Roll-off
Meanwhile long-running negotiations had been taking place with the local councils and port authorities on the proposal for a drive-through service to replace the *Loch Seaforth* on the age-old mail run from Stornoway to Kyle and Mallaig. Ullapool was not a railhead and the direct crossing from Stornoway was more exposed to the prevailing wind than the longer one to Kyle but on the principle of operating the shortest sea crossing Ullapool easily won the argument. As a stop-gap the *Iona* was given back to MacBrayne's to take over from the mailboat on the traditional route while end-loading terminals were constructed. Re-appearing with a red funnel, she took up the service in May 1972, although not on the traditional timings. Since she had no sleeping accommodation, unlike the *Loch Seaforth*, all sailings had to be during the day and her roster was consequently revamped. It was also accelerated to reflect her greater speed. Immediately the Freight Division started operating arcticulated lorries on their Glasgow-Stornoway route: they were loaded with great skill on to the *Iona's* hoist. The *Loch Seaforth* in turn moved to Oban to replace the *Claymore* on the Tiree and Barra'boisdale station: at a stroke pressure on this route was eased as she could carry more cars as deck cargo than the newer vessel. The *Claymore* was laid up in Greenock, temporarily as events turned out.

Further plans to increase the number of drive-through vessels were put into effect when the *Clansman* adjourned to Troon after her 1972 Armadale season for lengthening. She also had her passenger accommodation raised to give additional clearance on the car deck, and was fitted with a bow visor and stern door. The plan was to take over as Stornoway-Ullapool ferry once the terminals were in place.

As a stop-gap the *Iona* took over from the mailboat on the traditional route from Mallaig and Kyle to Stornoway in 1972; she is seen here at Stornoway, her funnel now painted red and black, in June 1973

J Aikman Smith

In 1972 the *Loch Seaforth* moved to Oban to work the Tiree and Barra'boisdale station; here she is seen at Coll loading a container into her cargo hold by her derrick in August of that year

J Aikman Smith

Caledonian MacBrayne

During this time momentous changes were taking place in the adminstration of the STG. Early in 1972, as part of the rationalisation process, a new unit called Caledonian MacBrayne Services was formed to maintain the fleets of both MacBrayne's and the CSP, although in all other aspects the two companies were to remain separate. On 1 January 1973, however, The Caledonian Steam Packet Co Ltd was renamed Caledonian MacBrayne Ltd and this 'new' company took over the shipping services of both the CSP and MacBrayne's. For a while David MacBrayne Ltd was retained to operate certain mail runs, cargo services and minor ferries (eight vessels in all), although the management was by Caledonian MacBrayne. MacBrayne's management and staff moved to the relatively new CSP headquarters at Gourock and the Robertson Street office was closed - some staff worked out of Portakabins until the offices could be suitably extended. Although the two fleets operated as one, complete integration between the two Divisions, Clyde and Western Isles, was slow and the ships' crews remained members of their existing trade unions, which were different.

Although the eight vessels retained by David MacBrayne Ltd retained their red and black funnels, the Caledonian MacBrayne (CalMac) ships had their funnels painted dark red with a yellow disc in the centre sporting a red 'CSP lion'. Initially they were owned by a subsidiary, Caledonian MacBrayne Holdings Ltd (the former Arran Piers Ltd taken over by the CSP in 1969). The MacBrayne flag with its double saltire now had the Caley lion added to it on a yellow disc.

A second new company, MacBrayne Haulage Ltd (Bute Ferry Co Ltd renamed), took over the management of MacBrayne's road freight services until sold off under instructions from the Government in 1985. In May 1973 they moved from their depot in Lancefield Street to a new purpose-built head office and depot in Blochairn Road, also in Glasgow. As the traditional cargo ships carried less and less MacBrayne Haulage, using the new hoist-loading and drive-through vessels, attracted an steadily increasing share of the island freight business. Both Caledonian MacBrayne and MacBrayne Haulage had the same Board of Directors. The Chairman for the first two years was Mr W Moris Little, who was already Managing Director of STG, and he was followed in 1975 by Mr Ian S Irwin. The General Manager was Mr N John D Whittle, who had been General Manager of the CSP since 1969. He subsequently became Executive Director and then Deputy Chairman of Caledonian MacBrayne Ltd. This was an enlightened management team and, while they made some decisions which were of necessity pragmatic rather than strategic, they carried the Company forward immeasurably in a very few years.

The Clyde Fleet

The CSP fleet in 1973 comprised thirteen vessels in service on the Clyde, two excursion steamers, two motor vessels carrying passengers only, five major car ferries and four small bow-loaders. The doyen of the fleet was the forty year old turbine steamer *Queen Mary II*, which mainly gave day excursions from Gourock to the far corners of the firth - Arran via the Kyles of Bute, Campbeltown and Inveraray. The other traditional ship was the paddle steamer *Waverley*, which gave

On the amalgamation with The Caledonian Steam Packet Co MacBrayne's management and staff moved to Gourock and their Robertson Street office was closed; the photograph shows Head Office in Robertson Street

The doyen of the CSP fleet was the forty year old turbine steamer Queen Mary II which mainly gave day excursions from Gourock to Arran,Campbeltown and Inveraray; she is seen here leaving Campbeltown in September 1973   *J Aikman Smith*

shorter cruises Round Bute, Round the Lochs and to Tarbert. Much was made of the fact that she was an historic vessel, reckoned to be the world's last sea-going paddler. One other CSP paddle steamer was based in Balloch and sailed on Loch Lomond. The *Maid of the Loch* (1953) had been transferred to a member company of the Scottish Bus Group, Alexander's, but she was still managed by CalMac.

The most modern car ferry was the *Caledonia*, bought as *Stena Baltica* three years previously and the Clyde's only truly drive-through vessel. She was on the busy 55 minute crossing between Ardrossan and Brodick in Arran. Larger, faster and more popular was the 1957 *Glen Sannox*, built for the Arran run but now converted to stern- and side-loading and operating between Gourock and Dunoon. She was assisted by a 'pup', the *Maid of Cumbrae*, a passenger vessel recently converted to a small, limited but still useful car ferry. Originally there had been four "*Maids*" on the Clyde but two were on the sale list in a Greenock Harbour while the *Maid of Argyll* was overhauled and retained as a spare vessel for passengers only.

There were originally three car ferries built for Clyde service in 1954, the *Arran*, *Bute* and *Cowal*, appropriately known as the ABC ferries. The *Arran* had already been transferred to the Western Isles and the other two were seeing out their twilight years sailing between Wemyss Bay and Rothesay on the Isle of Bute on an hourly frequency: this was still a hoist-loading operation. (The *Bute* was also used as a relief ship in the Western Isles.) The 'back door' to Bute across the narrow Kyles between Colintraive and Rhubodach was in the hands of two ferries which had formerly served Skye on the Kyle-Kyleakin route and had been converted to bow-loading, the *Portree* and *Broadford*. Similar bow-loaders which had originated in Skye sailed between Largs and Cumbrae Slip, the *Coruisk* and *Largs* (formerly *Kyleakin*); a coach connection was provided to the main township on the island, Millport. Arran too had a 'back door', opened in 1972 when a small landing craft vessel *Kilbrannan* inaugurated a summer only service between new slipways at Lochranza in the north west of Arran and Claonaig, near Skipness in Kintyre, in a sense a substitution for the mail run from Gourock to Tarbert and Ardrishaig. The last member of the fleet, the *Keppel*, provided a seasonal passenger only service direct from Largs to Millport Old Pier; this was a 30 minute rather than 10 minute crossing and was diminishing in popularity.

Replacing the former turntable Skye boats were two double-ended drive-through ferries each capable of carrying thirty cars, the *Kyleakin* and *Lochalsh*, dating from 1970 and 1971 respectively. Owned originally by the CSP, they were now part of the combined fleet. The queues which were so much part and parcel of the Kyle-Kyleakin route were now a thing of the past but as the decade wore on even the new ships were being stretched at peak periods.

A Series of Quick Solutions
Caledonian MacBrayne Ltd inherited some unfinished business from its two predecessors and as a consequence had an eventful first year or two. The STG's response to the newly found security of Western Ferries on the Islay route had been to withdraw the *Arran* completely on 30 December 1972 and have her fitted with a

In 1973 much was made of the fact that the *Waverley* was the world's last sea-going paddle steamer; she is seen here dressed overall at fleet headquarters at Gourock in September of that year

Graham E Langmuir

One other CSP paddler, the *Maid of the Loch*, was based at Balloch and sailed on Loch Lomond; she is seen here off Balmaha in August 1977　　　　　　　　*Lawrence J Macduff*

The *Glen Sannox* was built for the Arran run but was converted to stern- and side-loading and operated between Gourock and Dunoon; here she is seen on this service   *J Aikman Smith*

The *Maid of Cumbrae*, 'pup' on the Gourock-Dunoon service, calling specially at Rothesay; also berthed is the turbine Queen Mary II

In 1973 the *Maid of Argyll* was retained as a spare vessel; she is seen here at Tarbert deputising for P.S. *Waverley*, which had boiler trouble   *Ian MacKinnon*

A look back at Wemyss Bay around 1960 with the *Arran* loading cars for Rothesay and a larger passenger only vessel coping with the foot passengers at noon on a Saturday. The scene had hardly changed when CalMac took over

Two former Skye ferries *Broadford* (left) and *Largs* at the slip at Largs while on the Cumbrae service

Lawrence J Macduff

Arran had a 'back door' opened in 1972 when the small landing craft vessel *Kilbrannan* inaugurated a service between Lochranza and Kintyre; here she is loading at Lochranza in July of that year. She is sporting the yellow funnel of the CSP *J Aikman Smith*

new stern ramp for drive-on operation in place of her hoist and all superstructure aft. She returned to the fray in April 1973 to give three double runs daily between converted terminals at West Loch Tarbert and Port Ellen. She no longer called at Port Askaig or the other islands. The Group meantime ordered a new ro-ro ferry, the spin being that she was "for general work". Her shallow draught, however, suggested a specific sphere of operation and when the *Pioneer* appeared in August 1974 she indeed took over the Islay service from the *Arran*. Though her complement for passengers and cars was not significantly greater than the ship she replaced, her accommodation was superior and she was faster. With a Government subsidy behind her she was more than a match for Western Ferries' *Sound of Jura*. The red-hulled vessel gave her last run in August 1976 and was sold to Mexico, although the smaller *Sound of Islay* soldiered on for a few years.

When CalMac was formed the *Clansman* was undergoing radical alterations at Troon. She emerged in July 1973 scarcely recognisable and was rushed into service as the *Iona* on the Stornoway-Ullapool run had just suffered a major breakdown. By now linkspans had been installed at both Stornoway and Ullapool. When the *Clansman* arrived at Stornoway to take over she experienced a complete electrical failure but after this inauspicious start she settled down. Unfortunately she had not been re-engined during her conversion and was decidedly under-powered while at the same time her capacity was being really stretched when traffic peaked. The use of the *Clansman*, then, was not a long-term solution for the Stornoway service, although it did make the cargo ship *Lochdunvegan* redundant; when she happened to ground at Lochboisdale in August she was immediately placed on the disposal list. By good fortune there was a Norwegian vessel hardly a year old for sale, but when she was inspected more closely it was found that she would hardly comply with the rigorous safety standards set for British ships. By even greater fortune the keel of an identical twin was about to be laid and agreement was reached that this second ship should be transferred to CalMac and built from the outset to British standards. In August 1974, then, the *Suilven*, named appropriately after a prominent mountain in Sutherland, arrived in Scottish waters and promptly took her place on the Stornoway-Ullapool station. With her complement of cars at 120, thanks to two mezzanine decks, she solved at a stroke any capacity problems on the route and, although like her predecessor not exactly a greyhound, she gave sterling service on the route for the following twenty years.

At the start of 1973 the *Loch Seaforth* was on the route from Oban to Coll, Tiree, Barra and Lochboisdale. She immediately added Colonsay to her itinerary as with the temporary withdrawal of the *Arran* from the Islay route that island would otherwise have been cut off. The old mailboat's new career, however, came to an abrupt end in March when she struck a rock in the Sound of Gunna separating Coll from Tiree. She was towed into Tiree Pier but promptly sank the following morning, totally blocking the pier to all comers. The only vessel available to take over in the emergency was the *Claymore*, languishing in Greenock's East India Harbour. She was quickly reactivated and returned to her old haunts, using a flitboat at Tiree until the "*Seaforth*" could be lifted from the face of the pier by a floating crane, provided with temporary buoyancy and towed away to Troon for breaking up. The cargo boat

Replacing the turntable Skye boats were two double-ended drive-through ferries; the *Lochalsh*, seen here leaving Kyle of Lochalsh, dated from 1971

The *Arran*, after being fitted with a stern ramp, returned to the fray in 1973 to give three double runs daily between converted terminals at West Loch Tarbert and Port Ellen; she is seen here manœuvring off Port Ellen

When the *Pioneer* appeared in August 1974 she took over the Islay service; here she is seen creating a beautiful wave formation in West Loch Tarbert in September of that year *Lawrence J Macduff*

When CalMac was formed in 1973 the *Clansman* was undergoing radical alterations at Troon; she is seen here in late May nearing the end of her conversion to a drive-through ferry. In the background is the *Loch Seaforth* being broken up after her sinking at Tiree *J Aikman Smith*

Lochdunvegan assisted that summer in carrying cars to Tiree as the booked vehicles exceeded the capacity of the smaller *Claymore*. Meanwhile, in July, another redundant Stornoway ferry, the *Iona*, came to Oban to take over the car ferry service to Craignure, hanselling the new linkspan at Oban's Railway Pier in October. Her appearance allowed the *Columba* to move to Mallaig to fill the vacant space left by the *Clansman* on the crossing to Armdale together with the overnight service to Lochboisdale and Castlebay. The *Claymore's* trips to the Outer Isles were reduced in summer to one midweek.

Further improvements in the Western Isles were dependent on developments on the Clyde. Late in 1972, Western Ferries had purchased two basic roll-on roll-off ferries from Sweden together with land at Hunter's Quay, north of Dunoon. They also leased land at McInroy's Point, south of Gourock. They reconditioned the vessels, renaming them *Sound of Shuna* and *Sound of Scarba*, constructed two simple terminals and launched a service in opposition to CalMac in June. As in Islay five years previously, they captured a certain proportion of the traffic from the state company. At the same time the CSP had ordered from Lamont's of Port Glasgow two novel car ferries to be propelled not by conventional rudders and screws but by Voith-Schneider units fore and aft to give maximum manœuvrability. The first of the sisters, the *Jupiter*, was launched in November 1973 and was ready to take up service in March 1974. She was fitted with a stern ramp for use at Gourock and side ramps for Dunoon, where the linkspan was unusually along the face of the pier. Her ability to turn and berth was so efficient that she could achieve very fast turnrounds and was timetabled for an hourly service from each terminal.

It was in December 1973 that the *Juno* joined her sister *Jupiter* at Dunoon. This permitted the *Maid of Cumbrae* to be withdrawn from regular service but she continued to be used when required every time one of the new ships was taken off the run to transport gas tankers to Rothesay; in fact it was five years before she was sold out of the fleet. CalMac, incidentally, were now subsidised for their Clyde as well as their Western Isles services, otherwise new tonnage could never have been built. The Dunoon ferries were also employed on contract work with Admiralty workers between Gourock and Kilcreggan, the public service to that fairly isolated village being largely contracted out to a private operator, Roy Ritchie and later Clyde Marine Motoring, subsidised by Strathclyde Regional Council.

Another concern of Caledonian MacBrayne during their first year was the provision of Clyde cruising. The weather was particularly disappointing that season and traffic figures, especially in the longer full day excursions, plummeted. The other problem was the precarious state of the boilers of the paddle steamer *Waverley*. In November came the announcement that she was to be withdrawn from service. The turbine steamer *Queen Mary II* would in 1974 take over a combined roster incorporating the paddler's Round Bute and Round the Lochs trips together with one extended cruise to Brodick. A group of steamer enthusiasts, the Paddle Steamer Preservation Society, had formed a close liaison with STG in an effort to promote the uniqueness of the *Waverley* and in a magnificent gesture they were actually 'sold' the historic ship for a pound in August 1974. STG had assumed that the paddler would be

In August 1974 the *Suilven* arrived in Scottish waters from Norway and promptly took her place on the Stornoway-Ullapool station; she is seen passing Arnish Point, Isle of Lewis, in June 1975

Lawrence J Macduff

When the smaller *Claymore* was reactivated to take the place of the sunken *Loch Seaforth* on the Tiree run in 1973 the cargo boat *Lochdunvegan* assisted in carrying cars to Tiree; she is seen here loading at Oban's Railway Pier in July that year

preserved statically but her new owners, the Waverley Steam Navigation Co, through prodigious efforts raised enough money and harnessed sufficient volunteers to refit her, drydock her and return her to steam. Few dreamt that on 22 May 1975, the date of her second 'maiden' voyage, she would survive with colours flying past her Jubilee and into the next century.

Marine Motorways
The vessel displaced by the *Jupiter* at Dunoon was the *Glen Sannox*. She was therefore free to move round to Oban and succeed the *Iona* on the busy crossing to Craignure from late April 1974. The *Iona* in turn was able to start a new fast daily 'Marine Motorway' from Oban to Castlebay and Lochboisdale, berthing overnight in the Outer Isles. A linkspan was available at Lochboisdale from June and new freight business quickly developed. With her very early morning departures from South Uist, however, one disadvantage quickly became apparent - her lack of sleeping berths. This situation was remedied by adding a deckhouse aft of the officers' accommodation to provide eight four-berth cabins during her next overhaul (and at the same time removing her apology for a funnel and painting her exhausts, lengthened six feet, in Cal Mac colours). The coming of the *Iona* let the *Claymore* concentrate purely on the islands of Coll, Tiree and Colonsay and the *Columba* on Armadale, as her nocturnal voyages to the Outer Isles from Mallaig were no longer required. In winter the *Iona* was able to serve Coll and Tiree in addition and so the *Claymore* could at last be withdrawn from service.

The *Glen Sannox* did not in fact remain for long at Oban, at least in summer. When the *Suilven* was commissioned on the Stornoway crossing in August 1974 a cascade of vessels took place. The *Clansman* became the third Stornoway vessel to move south to Oban: she took her place briefly on the Mull ferry service that autumn but returned to it for the full 1975 season. The *Glen Sannox* was therefore able to return to the Clyde as one of the Wemyss Bay-Rothesay ferries, even at this stage still using her hoist; in addition she transported several hundred men daily to Ardyne on the south of the Cowal peninsula where Sir Robert McAlpine & Co were building huge concrete oil-rigs. She in turn displaced the *Bute*, which repaired to Troon for alterations to her hoist to enable her to cope with the extreme tidal range in her next employment. This was as Mallaig-Armadale ferry, which she became in May 1975. The *Columba* meanwhile had returned to Oban to take over as the summer boat to Coll, Tiree and Colonsay. In addition, however, she performed the excursion to Iona twice a week, sailing in each direction via the south of Mull and continuing northwards for a sight of Staffa. Using to the full the *Columba's* substantial sleeping accommodation, CalMac was able to offer these sailings as two- or three-day "Mini Cruises" which soon became very popular. The downside from the point of view of the public if not the Company accountant was that the veteran turbine *King George V* did not appear in the 1975 timetable. After almost fifty years giving pleasure to countless thousands of day trippers first on the Clyde and then out of Oban, the last Western Isles steamship had been taken out of service and placed on the sale list. The rôle of the one surviving cargo vessel *Loch Carron* diminished every time a route was adapted to drive-through operation: she sailed for the last time under the Company's flag in November 1976 by which time MacBrayne's had permission to

The first of the Clyde sisters for Gourock-Dunoon, the *Jupiter*, was launched in November 1973 and was ready to take up service in March 1974; she is seen here on trials at the Tail of the Bank. In her first year the bulwarks at the stern were painted white and GOUROCK-DUNOON ferry was written large on the hull   *James Hall*

The *Iona*, altered for her new employment on the Marine Motorway to the Outer Isles, seen here berthed at Castlebay, Isle of Barra   *Lawrence J Macduff*

An action shot of the *Bute*, the new Mallaig-Armadale ferry, as she nears Armadale in June 1975

Lawrence J Macduff

The last surviving cargo vessel *Loch Carron* passing under the new Erskine Bridge in July 1974

Graham E Langmuir

withdraw the last direct sailing from the Clyde, 125 years after Hutcheson's had originally taken over.

Island Class
In the first two years of the Company's existence, CalMac had commissioned four major ro-ro ferries and had disposed of six of their ships. While the major routes were largely converted to drive-through operation, the smaller islands were treated in an equally revolutionary way. Following on from the *Kilbrannan* which had joined the CSP fleet in 1972, seven more small bow-loading ferries, known as the Small Island Class and able to carry five or six cars and about fifty passengers, had been built by 1976. The *Morvern* had been ordered by STG at the same time as the *Kilbrannan* but did not appear on the scene till April 1973. She inaugurated the service for which she was named, namely between Lochaline in Morvern and Fishnish, the nearest point in Mull, just at the time when the *Columba* had been transferred to Skye and her replacement as Mull ferry no longer continued to Lochaline. Just before this time there had been much activity at the jetties at Iona and at Fionnphort, directly across the Sound at the tip of the Ross of Mull. MacBraynes' had had a fleet of 'red boats' there since 1933 to ferry passengers ashore from the Oban cruise steamer; since October 1972 one of the little boats also looked after the crossing from Fionnphort, even shipping vehicles and livestock when the occasion demanded. Now the *Morvern* took over this latter duty but so that the Sacred Isle could retain some of its tranquillity tourists had to leave their cars behind and proceed by foot, only islanders' cars and commercial vehicles being allowed to board.

Both the *Kilbrannan* and *Morvern* were soon found to be slightly too small - an extra five feet would have made all the difference to their carrying capacity. The next of the class to appear, in June 1973, was the *Bruernish*, and she was in fact that little bit longer. She initially took over from the *Morvern* but like her she was used on various routes - including a charter from Kyleakin to the Howard Doris oil platform being constructed in nearby Loch Kishorn - until she too became established on one crossing. In February 1979 she was called upon to provide a service from West Loch Tarbert to Gigha, loading by crane, but Gigha and Tayinloan, directly opposite in Kintyre, soon had slipways and she became ensconced in her new station. The fourth Island Class ferry, the *Rhum*, took over from the smaller *Kilbrannan* on the Lochranza-Claonaig service in June 1973 and remained there. The *Kilbrannan* was demoted to the status of relief vessel on the Largs-Cumbrae Slip service until June 1977 when she became the Scalpay ferry sailing from Kyles Scalpay in Harris, relegating the *Scalpay* to the sale list. (This *Scalpay* was actually the second of the name; a former Skye ferry, she had taken up the run in 1971). The final member of the first batch of new ships was the *Coll*, which, after a spell relieving the *Loch Arkaig* on the Small Isles route starting in November 1973, spent three years working between Lochaline and Fishnish before spending a year at Loch Kishorn and then becoming the spare and relief vessel for her class.

There followed a gap in construction until the *Eigg* appeared over a year later. CalMac had decided that the two services entrusted to the *Loch Arkaig*, the Small

The *Morvern* inaugurated the service for which she was named, namely between Lochaline in Morvern and Fishnish, the nearest point in Mull; she is seen here unloading a cargo of sheep at Lismore. In the background is the converted car ferry *Clansman* on the Craignure run   *J Aikman Smith*

The third Island Class ferry, *Bruernish*, was employed on various routes in the 1970s; here she is seen on a special chartered sailing at Inverie in Loch Nevis   *J Aikman Smith*

Isles run from Mallaig and the Raasay and Portree run from Kyle, should be separated on grounds of efficiency, with the *Loch Arkaig* concentrating on the Small Isles section and an Island Class ferry placed on the crossing between Raasay and Sconser, fifteen minutes away on Skye. The construction of a slipway on Raasay, however, was delayed by the refusal of the absentee landlard, Dr Green, to sell the required land. In February 1975 the *Eigg* inaugurated a service from Portree, run for passengers only using the conventional piers. She did not remain long on this station, however, and soon moved to Oban and settled down as the Lismore ferry. (It had been in 1964 that the Lismore passenger launch *Lochnell* and the Kyle-Toscaig-Kylerhea ferry *Loch Toscaig* had exchanged places; the latter had remained on the Lismore run till 1974, after which she had eventually been withdrawn. Island class vessels had then maintained the service each on a short-term basis.) Taking the *Eigg's* place at Raasay in January 1976 was the seventh Island Class ferry *Canna*. On Good Friday that year she hanselled the new slipway at Sconser and from that date calls at Portree ceased after 125 years, although the harbour was still to feature on occasions as a cruise destination. The *Canna* was relieved in July 1976 by the last of the series, the *Raasay*, which, appropriately, remained for many years. She herself moved to Lochaline, originally as spare vessel but latterly as the dedicated ferry.

Clyde Improvements
1978 saw the completion of CalMac's initial modernisation programme on the Clyde. By 1976 it had become apparent that the busy Ardrossan-Arran was being served by the relatively small *Caledonia* while the spacious *Clansman*, with 50% more capacity, was sailing with relatively light loadings between Oban and Mull. CalMac decided that the sensible action would be to switch the two ships in summer. This measure was very effective. Gradually, with traffic increasing year on year, the *Caledonia's* winter passenger certificate proved ever more inadequate and so the *Clansman* started to spend more and more time on the Clyde, despite her lack of ability to manœuvre in Ardrossan Harbour. Mull was in turn served by the *Glen Sannox* which sailed north every winter, at least from 1977. The Mull roster incorporated a thrice-weekly voyage to Colonsay in winter and so it could not be operated by the *Caledonia* as she had no hoist.

The flotilla of small vessels operating between Largs and Cumbrae Slip was subject to breakdowns and queues of cars frequently built up on each side. Just as in Skye six years previously, the solution was to order one large purpose-built ship. Such a vessel, a smaller edition of the *Kyleakin* and *Lochalsh*, appeared in April 1977. The *Isle of Cumbrae* was of great benefit to the islanders and delays now occurred only at the very busiest holiday periods. The *Coruisk* and *Largs* were retained in a spare and relief capacity for a few years while the passenger vessel *Keppel* continued to sail round to Millport Old Pier.

Rothesay too benefited from new tonnage. Linkspans, conventional at Wemyss Bay and along the face of the pier at Rothesay, were at last introduced in May/June 1977. At the same time the Ardyne contract came to an end as McAlpine's had failed to maintain a full order book and so the *Glen Sannox* was able to become the main

In July 1976 the last of the Island Class ferries, *Raasay*, took over the Raasay-Sconser service; she remained on it for many years and is here seen at the Raasay terminal in July 1997

J Roderick McCrorie

The *Caledonia* switched places with the larger *Clansman* in summer from 1976 for capacity reasons; here she is seen passing the Hutcheson Monument on Kerrera as she nears Oban *Lawrence J Macduff*

The *Clansman* in turn became the Ardrossan-Brodick ferry; she is seen here at Brodick with Goatfell in the background in June 1976   *J Aikman Smith*

One large purpose-built ship to replace the flotilla of small vessels operating between Largs and Cumbrae Slip appeared in April 1977; here is the *Isle of Cumbrae* approaching Largs with the *Coruisk* anchored off

Rothesay ferry, making full use of her stern ramp at Wemyss Bay. The faithful *Cowal*, having outlived her usefulness, was sold to the Greeks. A month later the *Saturn*, purpose-built for the service, was launched at Troon but because of problems with the alignments of her shafts it was not until February in the following year that she made her inaugural trip on the crossing. A quasi-sister of the *Jupiter* and *Juno*, she incorporated several improvements, not least the high level bridge and a tripod mainmast rising from the after end of the upper deck rather than the tetrapod mast rising from the funnel at main deck level, a rather cumbersome arrangement.

In the winter of 1976/77 the *Glen Sannox* had been re-engined and completely refurbished and upgraded at Hall, Russell's in Aberdeen. This was to equip her to maintain a double life as a car ferry in winter and at peak periods in summer but for the rest of the time to act as a cruise vessel, seemingly a very sensible course of action economically. By now the veteran turbine *Queen Mary II* had been competing with the paddle steamer *Waverley* for three seasons. Despite generous grants from Strathclyde Regional Council and a publicity campaign culminating in her dropping the '*II*' from her name, despite being the faster and roomier vessel and even returning to the centre of Glasgow where she had sailed with great success in her earlier days, she could not compete in the public eye with the nostalgia inherent in the "last sea-going paddle steamer in the world". It was woefully uneconomic for CalMac to retain an expensive steamer for summer-only excursion duties and so, albeit reluctantly, the Management laid up their last turbine in September 1977. With the *Saturn* commissioned on the Rothesay route the *Glen Sannox* was free to take over for the 1978 season. This left the *Maid of the Loch* on Loch Lomond as the only steamship operated by CalMac. She had just two years previously received a thorough overhaul of her passenger accommodation and machinery and had been the object of a new publicity drive; her roster was recast following advice from marketing consultants. As a result her passenger numbers for a while showed a definite increase.

While the "*Sannox*" was much more economical to operate than the "*Mary*", was employed throughout the year and had been refurbished to the highest modern standards, inflation was high, local authority support was waning, poor summer followed poor summer and there was no contest in the public's mind between a steam paddler and a diesel car ferry. It was inevitable that after only four seasons the *Glen Sannox* was withdrawn from Clyde cruising. She then became spare in summer but continued to operate out of Oban in winter. The *Maid of the Loch* suffered the same fate, perhaps just altogether too large and expensive for an inland loch steamer. While Loch Lomond was undoubtedly one of the most exquisite beauty spots in the country there were no resorts like Rothesay, Millport or Tobermory for the day tripper of the late twentieth century to visit and that made marketing just a bit more difficult.

A Cascade of Vessels
The modernisation programme in the Western Isles was all but complete in 1976 but the CalMac policies had been so successful that traffic continued to increase relentlessly. The routes which were specially under-resourced were the long haul

It was in February 1978 that the *Saturn* made her inaugural trip on the crossing between Rothesay and Wemyss Bay

It was in January 1979 that the *Claymore* was commissioned on the Isles run from Oban; she is seen here in the evening going astern into Lochboisdale, South Uist

from Oban to Barra'boisdale and the Islay service, although the latter received a fillip when STG bought the Western Ferries' terminal at Kennacraig and the *Pioneer* was able to operate from there from 1978, thus cutting vital minutes off each journey. At the same time the terminal at Port Ellen was extended.

It was in January 1979 that a new ferry was commissioned on the Isles run from Oban. This was the *Claymore*, from the same stable as the *Pioneer*, Robb Caledon of Leith, and in many ways a development of the 1974 ship, though considerably larger. She served Castlebay/Lochboisdale and Coll/Tiree on alternate days, using her stern ramp at Oban and Lochboisdale and her hoist at all other ports. In summer, of course, with the *Columba* available, she could concentrate on the heavy schedule to and from the Outer Isles. Traffic congestion was relieved but even the *Claymore* had to supplement her roster at certain times to facilitate the movement of army traffic to the Uists.

Yet a further cascade of vessels took place on the commissioning of the *Claymore*. The *Iona* was now free to take up the Islay service as the Secretary of State had proposed ten years before, especially now that Port Ellen had been extended and the mainland terminal moved to Kennacraig, where there was deep water. This she did in February 1979. The *Iona* was too deep-draughted to call at the pier on Gigha as the *Arran* and *Pioneer* had done and that was why the Island Class ferry *Bruernish* commenced a service to Gigha at the same time. When Western Ferries finally abandoned their opposition service to Port Askaig with the *Sound of Islay* in September 1981, Islay was served by the *Iona* alone, although the *Sound of Gigha* was retained for the ancillary service to Jura. Port Askaig calls now gradually returned to the CalMac timetable. The *Pioneer*, now displaced, returned to her birthplace and emerged in May complete with a hoist with four large lift supports just abaft her funnels. This was needed for her new employment as Mallaig-Armadale ferry in summer and relief ship, mainly on the Clyde, in winter. The *Bute*, which was at Mallaig the previous summer, was sold to Greece. The last of the original trio of CSP car ferries, the *Arran*, had been retained as spare vessel for almost five years. There was now no need for her in the fleet and so she too was sold, becoming a floating restaurant in Dublin for some time.

The last new tonnage of the seventies was a replacement for the *Loch Arkaig*, a product of 1941 and now rather down at heel. She no longer sailed to Raasay and Portree but concentrated on the service from Mallaig to the Small Isles of Eigg, Muck, Rum and Canna. The last named was the only island to possess a pier; at the others passengers, livestock and cargo had to be taken ashore by flitboat. Because of this and because of the very exposed nature of the crossing, especially in winter, it was not easy to design a suitable successor and quite a controversy arose among the various interested parties. Tenders were invited for an 84 foot vessel and, although an order was placed with Ailsa of Troon, CalMac was not happy with the specification. At the end of the day, however, the Government announced that the length was to be increased to 102 feet and as a consequence the summer complement was raised from 80 to 120. The *Lochmor* appeared in July 1979, not a moment too soon as the *Loch Arkaig* had sunk at her berth at Mallaig four months beforehand

The *Iona* became free to take up the Islay service in 1979, especially as the mainland terminal had moved to Kennacraig, where there was deep water; here she is seen at Kennacraig in June 1981

The *Pioneer*, complete with a hoist, was employed as Mallaig-Armadale ferry from 1979; here she is seen at Mallaig in June that year

J Aikman Smith

and had had to be sold. The new trim little craft could carry two cars on her open main deck aft and had fairly comfortable, if basic, passenger accommodation. She had a dual function both as a lifeline to the islands and as a ship for tourists: in her early days she carried out trips to Kyle and farther north, including Portree, in between her voyages to the Small Isles.

Political Scrutiny

The early eighties saw a lull in the building of new ships. STG through their subsidiary had achieved most of their ambitions, although there were still some routes to be converted to ro-ro. With an annual subsidy now in excess of £5 million, it was of course right that the Company should be strictly accountable and that any measures to bring about economies should be regularly sought. During this period, then, the Company came under political scrutiny. In July 1981, for example, the Conservative Secretary of State controversially proposed in the House of Commons that the subsidy for CalMac's Gourock-Dunoon run be withdrawn and a capital grant offered to Western Ferries in lieu so that they could buy another ferry for their opposition service. In addition the private company was to provide an initially subsidised passenger service from Dunoon Pier using their fast craft *Highland Seabird*, which was lying idle at the time. STG had no alternative but to announce that they would withdraw from Dunoon at the end of the summer timetable. Just as in Islay a decade before Cowal erupted in fury and 376 objections were lodged against the proposal. The result of the subsequent public enquiry was that "serious hardship, inconvenience and difficulty" would be caused if CalMac withdrew as the *Highland Seabird* could not be relied upon to provide a service, especially in winter. Eventually, in February 1982, the Secretary of State declared that CalMac would receive a passenger only subsidy for their Gourock-Dunoon route but they would have to compete with Western Ferries for vehicle traffic on a commercial basis. Western Ferries were distinctly upset by the decision as they had just announced their intention to purchase an additional ferry on the basis of the Government's promise the previous year and feared bankruptcy. CalMac, on the other hand, had to operate their service at the frequency of one sailing per hour, with a modest enhancement allowed at peak commuter times. This restriction ensured that their subsidy would not be used to force Western Ferries off the Hunter's Quay-McInroy's Point route.

The same year a Government committee issued a report stating that there was scope for tighter control of CalMac's finances. This was the catalyst for the subsequent announcement that CalMac was to be investigated by the Monopolies and Mergers Commission which would examine their costs and efficiency route by route with respect to the annual subsidy. The Commission reported in February 1983 and commended the high level of service and reliability offered by the CalMac ships. They did, however, make several recommendations. Two bow-loading ferries plus the *Keppel* were to be withdrawn; either the *Jupiter* or *Juno* was to be immediately disposed of as only one was needed for the Dunoon service and the revenue from the RNAD Kilcreggan contract was not enough to break even; the Tobermory-Mingary link (maintained by the *Lochnell* between 1968 and 1980 and thereafter by the red boat *Applecross*) was to be investigated; surcharges were to be introduced to avoid

The trim little craft *Lochmor* slipped for overhaul on Goat Island, Stornoway, in February 1992

In July 1981 it was proposed that the subsidy for CalMac's Gourock-Dunoon run be withdrawn; here the *Saturn* is about to leave Gourock for Dunoon   *J Roderick McCrorie*

high peaks in demand; a full time Chief Executive was to be appointed; and masters of the major vessels were to have more responsibility for their own routes. The reaction from the public was generally hostile, as it had been compiled by accountants and had taken no account of the social element inherent in the CalMac service. At the end of the day there was little immediate effect. The small bow-loader *Largs* was indeed withdrawn as stand-by Cumbrae ferry at the end of 1983 but the *Keppel* was retained for a while and the Secretary of State gave permission for the *Jupiter* to be kept in the fleet as well. Fares were restructured and a new Chief Executive, Colin Paterson, was appointed in July 1983.

Major New Additions
At this point the first new tonnage for four years entered the fleet. The *Isle of Arran*, built by Ferguson Ailsa of Port Glasgow, took over the Ardrossan-Brodick route in April 1984. Her predecessor, the *Clansman*, was slow and unwieldy, though with good accommodation, while her winter relief, the *Caledonia*, frequently embarrassed the Company by her small passenger carrying capacity. The new ship's complement was only slightly less than the *Clansman* in summer but three times that of the *Caledonia* in winter. Her service speed of 15 knots also allowed her to complete the journey in the scheduled 55 minutes. Although the first STG service to be converted to ro-ro, the Ardrossan-Arran run had never been entirely satisfactory; now with its first purpose-built vessel that situation had been remedied. The *Isle of Arran* had a very successful season and quickly endeared herself to the Arran travellers. She was well furnished, two innovations being her No Smoking lounge and her invalid lift from car deck to passenger accommodation. The *Clansman* was sold out of the fleet in August.

It was at the launch of the *Isle of Arran* that the Secretary of State announced that £7 million was to be spent on a replacement for the *Hebrides* on the run from Uig to Tarbert and Lochmaddy and a further £5 million on modification to the terminals for ro-ro operation. The 'Uig triangle', as the route was called, offered access to North and South Uist via Lochmaddy and Harris and Lewis via Tarbert and right from the outset STG considered it to be the natural candidate to be principal route to the Outer Isles. This stategy, however, was frustrated largely because of lack of finance from the local authorities which owned two of the piers and partly because of the lack of willingness of the islanders to change. Meanwhile the *Hebrides* continued on the station for several years but, because of the restrictions imposed by hoist-loading, she frequently ran very late when she was fully loaded and missed out on much of the heavy goods vehicle traffic which was conveyed instead via Lochboisdale or Stornoway, both with drive-through facilities. She was therefore unable to fulfil her revenue potential. An economic study promoted by CalMac had concluded back in 1979 that the potential was indeed there if ro-ro operation could be secured. The target date was 1985 but red tape delayed the process so that it was not until March 1984 that the contract for the new ship was awarded to an English yard which had given the lowest tender, Cochrane's of Selby, on the River Ouse. Extensive pier works were started at Lochmaddy and Tarbert but Uig Pier required an additional grant and this meant further delays.

The *Isle of Arran* took over the Ardrossan-Brodick route in April 1984; here she is seen leaving Ardrossan that month. In subsequent years the level of black paint on her hull was lowered and she looked more attractive   *Graham E Langmuir*

The *Hebridean Isles* set new standards for passenger accommodation when she appeared on the Uig triangle in May 1986   *Hamish M Stewart*

Because of the narrowness of the river the *Hebridean Isles* had to be launched sideways; the ceremony was performed in July 1985 by a member of the royal family, HRH the Duchess of Kent, the first time CalMac had received such an honour. Under the new régime, incidentally, all new major vessels had to have *"Isle"* or *"Isles"* in their name. The ship set new standards for passenger accommodation. She could load her vehicles by bow or stern ramp or by hoist, so that she could also serve on routes not converted to drive-through operation. On each side of her hull was the emblem of the EEC to acknowledge the Community's contribution to her building costs: she was in fact the first vessel to have access to the European Regional Development Fund. The *Hebridean Isles* was delivered late in 1985 but had to spend the winter relieving on other stations while the terminals a least at Lochmaddy and Tarbert were completed. The pioneer MacBrayne car ferry *Hebrides* was withdrawn in November and was given a rousing and sentimental send off. She was subsequently sold to Torbay Seaways and her sister *Columba* took over for the winter. Her replacement was able to appear at last on the Uig triangle in May 1986 but unforeseen civil engineering problems at Uig meant that she had to hoist-load there for her first eight months. Significant traffic growth then resulted and although some came from Lochboisdale and Stornoway much was totally new business. It had taken STG seventeen years to achieve this outcome.

"Loch" Class

By now traffic had built up on some of the minor routes so much that the fleet of Island Class vessels dating from the seventies could not cope. In addition CalMac still had several other small bow-loaders in service and they were now outdated. In July 1985 two new twelve-car 200-passenger ferries were ordered from Richard Dunston's of Hessle for delivery the following summer. Following her launch and fitting out the first of the pair, the *Loch Striven*, sailed from the Humber round the north of Scotland and through the Caledonian Canal to take up service between Largs and Cumbrae in July 1986, initially along with the *Isle of Cumbrae*, to give a fifteen minute service. The second to be completed, the *Loch Linnhe*, had a similar voyage but interrupted it at Lochaline to take over the Fishnish service from the *Canna*. A month later she and the *Isle of Cumbrae* changed places and the latter became the dedicated ferry on the 'back door' route to Mull. The Cumbrae service now had a much increased frequency and the Lochaline-Fishnish route was trebled in capacity. The spare Cumbrae ferry *Coruisk* was sold out of the fleet and the age-old service between Largs and Millport ceased, the *Keppel* being placed on a leisurely programme of inter-resort cruising on the Firth of Clyde. At the same time the *Canna* became spare and the *Coll* switched to Tobermory-Mingary to take over the seasonal service from the ferry boat *Applecross* and give a more robust facility. The latter had been withdrawn at the end of the previous season. Two more sisters were now on order from Dunstan's. The *Loch Riddon* took up the service between Colintraive and Rhubodach in October 1986 allowing the *Portree* and *Broadford* to be sold. Finally came the *Loch Ranza* which replaced the *Rhum* on the Lochranza-Claonaig station in April 1987; this Island Class ferry joined the *Canna* in a spare boat capacity. Thanks to the arrival of four 12-car ferries a total of five routes now had an enhanced level of service, cruising of a sort had been reintroduced to the Clyde and four older vessels had been withdrawn.

Mini-Liners

CalMac had by now decided that the next major improvement had to be on the Oban-Craignure service where the *Caledonia*, comfortable as she was, was not coping with the huge traffic peaks characteristic of the route in summer. The 1000 departure from Oban and the 1700 from Craignure were in the habit of 'boiling over' during a good spell of weather as they connected into very popular coach tours for Fionnphort and ferry to Iona or private launch to Staffa. An order was placed with Appledore-Ferguson's of Port Glasgow in June 1986 and so the Company could afford to withdraw the *Caledonia* at the end of the 1987 season. Following her launch by HRH Princess Alexandra, the *Isle of Mull* was duly introduced to the Mull route in April 1988 but, though perfectly safe and with truly magnificent accommodation, she suffered from a major capacity problem. Her inability to lift the required cargo deadweight necessitated her lengthening by 5.4 metres to meet her contractual requirements - to be paid for by the shipyard. After her first season, which was otherwise completely successful, she was taken to Middlesborough, drydocked, cut in two immediately forward of the funnel and had a new prefabricated section fitted between the two halves - all within a week. She was back in service in December and as a new linkspan had just been installed in Colonsay she was able to serve the two islands, Colonsay and Mull. The *Glen Sannox* was no longer required to fulfil this duty in winter. With capacity for 80 cars, 1000 passengers in summer and 600 in winter traffic problems were a thing of the past. Possibly thanks to the increased capacity of the *Isle of Mull* traffic was so heavy at Iona that the *Canna* had to be used as a backup for the *Morvern* on the ferry crossing.

The public had been aware since 1985 that CalMac planned to build a new ship for the Outer Isles run from Oban which would double as the Coll and Tiree ferry, thus reducing the number of vessels in service by one and effecting much-needed economies. The contract was again won by Appledore-Ferguson of Port Glasgow and was signed in June 1987 for completion in two years. The vessel to be withdrawn as a result was the *Columba* and this was realised at the end of the 1988 season. The loss of the *Columba* was felt quite deeply because it also signalled the end of the day cruise to Iona which had been carried out by the Company or its predecessors since 1851. Colonsay would also have to be served differently. The *Columba* was actually sold for further service. The following year, transformed into a cruise liner and renamed *Hebridean Princess*, she gave a programme of cruises from Oban to the Hebrides for a clientele clearly at the very top end of the market.

The new vessel *Lord of the Isles* was launched in March 1989 by the wife of the then Secretary of State for Scotland and on trial two months later proved herself to be at 16.85 knots easily the fastest vessel in the fleet. Smaller than the *Isle of Mull*, she nevertheless could still carry almost 60 cars and over 500 passengers. Unlike her consort she had an open stern and as only three of her regular ports of call had linkspans she was fitted also with a hoist. (The linkspan at Castlebay, Barra, had just been installed.) She took up service in late May and soon was on her arduous summer timetable which involved her sailing seven days a week, fitting in six trips to Barra'boisdale and four to Coll and Tiree. The *Claymore*, displaced after over ten

The first of the "Loch" class vessels, *Loch Striven*, sailed through the Caledonian Canal to take up service on the Clyde; here she is seen leaving the locks at Fort Augustus in June 1986

Graham E Langmuir

The *Isle of Mull* was introduced to the Oban-Craignure route in April 1988; here she is seen before she was lengthened at the end of the season to cure capacity problems   *J Aikman Smith*

years on the run, sailed for the Clyde to be refurbished to the standard of the newest vessels and altered slightly to equip her for her new duty, that of Islay ferry. The roster was revamped and now included a late afternoon sail to Colonsay on Mondays and a completely novel Kennacraig-Port Askaig-Colonsay-Oban day trip on Wednesdays, as a consequence of the withdrawal of the *Columba*. The *Iona*, with her hoist extended like the *Bute's* in the previous decade, became Mallaig-Armadale ferry, giving an additional weekly sailing on Sundays to Castlebay, a practice which had been revived by the *Pioneer* the previous year. The *Pioneer* herself did appear back at Mallaig in the early season but on the appearance of the *Iona* sailed round to the Clyde to have her hoist removed and replaced by simple side ramps. This was to allow her to load at the linkspans at Dunoon and Rothesay as she was now spare vessel for the fleet and Upper Clyde relief in winter. This rôle had belonged to the *Glen Sannox* and the 1957 veteran could now be sold - to the Greeks. There was genuine regret at her departure.

Transfer to the Secretary of State

While these far-reaching devolpments were taking place, controversy surrounded the very existence of CalMac. The Secretary of State announced in Parliament early in 1988 that he had decided in principle to privatise the Scottish Bus Group, the main subsidiary of STG, and was considering very closely the future of Caledonian MacBrayne. Public and press jumped to the conclusion that this would involve CalMac also in a degree of privatisation and the islanders especially worried if a privately owned company could maintain the same quality of service without a clearly unacceptable additional subsidy. It was November before the announcement was made that CalMac was to be kept as a single entity and would remain in public ownership but with its shares transferred to the Secretary of State. The Government would then own the Company directly rather than through STG. A new Board of Directors was to be appointed enjoined to improve efficiency, to examine the possibility of transferring the Dunoon and Rothesay routes to private ownership and to consider whether CalMac headquarters should be moved away from Gourock, say, to Oban. The change eventually occurred on 2 April 1990, the new chairman being Mr A J (Sandy) Struthers with Mr Colin Paterson continuing as Managing Director. Just over a year later the Government finally announced that the possible privatisation of the sheltered water ferries to Dunoon and Rothesay had been dropped or at least deferred, while the possible move of HQ to Oban had been rejected. There was general rejoicing at Gourock.

The Road to Skye

1990 was a year of planning. CalMac had to respond to the huge increase in car traffic to Skye, against the backdrop of the proposed Skye Bridge, due for completion in five years; linkspans had to be introduced to the remaining islands if hoist-loading were to be finally phased out; and some of the Island Class vessels had to be replaced by larger ships because of the continuing build up of traffic. During the year the Board was considering various options for the future. Coll and Tiree could be served six days a week from Tobermory in the same way as the Uists and Harris lifeline was from Uig, the problems being the infrastructure on Mull with its notorious single-track roads and the capacity problems which would result on the

The withdrawal of the *Columba* at the end of the 1988 season signalled the end of the day cruise to Iona; she is seen here arriving in the Sound in June 1975 *J Aikman Smith*

The *Lord of the Isles* took up her arduous summer timetable in May 1989; here she is seen berthing at Coll in April 1998 *IMcC*

The *Claymore*, displaced after ten years on the Isles run from Oban, became Islay ferry in 1989; here she is seen in the Sound of Islay nearing Port Askaig in June of that year   *J Aikman Smith*

With the commissioning of the *Lord of the Isles* in 1989 a cascade of vessels took place and the veteran car ferry *Glen Sannox* was withdrawn; she is seen here in happier days in May 1987 on a special excursion at Stranraer with Sealink's *St David* in the background   *IMcC*

143

Mull ferry, despite her large complement. The obstacles in this case proved too great and the idea was stillborn. Talks were taking place on the feasibility of a link across the mouth of Loch Fyne between Tarbert and Portavadie. Government permission was granted to operate the seasonal Tobermory-Mingary route, now restyled Tobermory-Kilchoan, as a vehicular ferry, thus giving a huge boost to Ardnamurchan and, along with Fishnish-Lochaline, offering a new route for tourists. The modernisation programme demanded that two new ships similar to the *Isle of Mull* be built for Arran and Stornoway while two smaller "Loch" class vessels, as they were called, would also be required, one for Iona. At the end of the year permission was indeed granted to invite tenders for a £2 million new vessel for Iona with a capacity almost double that of the *Morvern*.

The contract for the new Skye Bridge was awarded in April - ten days later CalMac introduced 24 hour working on the Skye ferries, which prompted some islanders to rethink the need for a toll bridge in the first place. A month earlier the first of the new generation of ferries, the *Loch Dunvegan*, had been launched at Ferguson's of Port Glasgow and in mid-May she entered service. Her capacity of 36 cars and 250 passengers meant that she was in a different league from the *Lochalsh* which she replaced. Despite teething problems with her ramp and fears that her high superstructure would impede navigation in windy conditions she settled in successfully. When joined by her sister *Loch Fyne* in early August the problem of capacity on the busy route had been solved. The *Isle of Cumbrae* appeared in winter to relieve the new ferries and act as an emergency stand-by ship. One condition with which CalMac had had to comply before finance for the new ships had been forthcoming was that they were capable of being redeployed when they became redundant on the completion of the bridge.

Both the *Kyleakin* and the *Lochalsh* were subsequently sold for further service in Eire. It is of interest that at the same time as the *Lochalsh* was voyaging across the Irish Sea the original Island Class ferry *Kilbrannan* was commmencing a two month charter in Donegal. She had been supplanted as Scalpay ferry by the *Canna* in 1990 and had been relegated to spare ferry. The *Rhum* had replaced the *Canna* as second vessel at Iona. The other event concerning the small vessels in 1991 was that, following the provision of new slipways at Tobermory and Kilchoan, the *Coll* did start providing a car ferry service between these two points. This was a very positive result of the "investigation" ordered by the Monopolies Commission back in 1983.

Small Ship Changes
Small vessels and Mull proved newsworthy also in 1992. The first of two ferries ordered from Miller's yard at St Monans in Fife, the *Loch Buie*, entered service in June. She was, as agreed, destined for Iona. A vessel of her size and capacity could scarcely have been imagined a few years before on the route from Fionnphort. As before, vehicles were severely restricted and it was of little consequence that a spacious passenger lounge, together with the navigating bridge, was placed athwartships thus making it impossible for a high vehicle to drive straight through the car deck. The *Morvern* now took the place of the *Kilbrannan* as spare vessel and the latter was sold for further service in the Irish Republic, on the Aranmore-

The *Loch Dunvegan* entered service as a Skye ferry in mid-May 1991; one of the previous generation of ferries, the *Kyleakin*, is in the background   *J Aikman Smith*

A vessel of the size and capacity of the *Loch Buie* could scarcely have been imagined as she loads up day excurisonists at the slip at Iona   *IMcC*

Burtonport crossing where she had gone on charter a year before. The *Morvern* followed four years later. The *Rhum* became spare and was laid up during the season.

The second vessel planned in 1990 and the second ordered from St Monans came into service in July. This was the *Loch Tarbert*, an 18-car ferry destined for the seasonal Lochranza-Claonaig service, where the *Loch Ranza* was having problems coping at peak periods. The queues evaporated. The *Loch Ranza* in turn had been promised to Gigha, where the small bow-loading vessel was having difficulty in accommodating some of the large vehicles used by the island's farmers. The slipways, however, had not yet been adapted and it was late September before she could take over. The *Bruernish* then became relief vessel.

1992 also saw the introduction of linkspans at Coll and Tiree so that the timetable of the *Lord of the Isles* could be appreciably accelerated. The season, however, suffered from indifferent weather and as a result one facility was to come to an end. CalMac's Clyde cruising vessel, the *Keppel*, although small and slow, had provided a service, especially for pensioners, for seven years sailing from Gourock, Helensburgh, Kilcreggan, Dunoon, Rothesay and Largs to Tighnabruaich in the Kyles of Bute, or Millport on Cumbrae. She had even run excursions to the Glasgow Garden Festival in 1988. Her carryings, already meagre, were well down and strong rumours circulated that she would not sail again for the Company after the 1992 summer. No grants were available to help and so in December her withdrawal was confirmed. After a disastrous season sailing out of Greenock for a private operator on 'Booze Cruises' etc. she was sold to Maltese interests. CalMac cruising was actually resumed the following season when one of the *Jupiter* class, affectionately known as "streakers" because of their ability to manœuvre so adeptly, used the slack period in the middle of the day between the busy commuter runs to offer a trip to Tighnabruaich two days per week. Encouraged by very cheap fares - only £2.50 for pensioners - the excursion was so well patronised that it had to be extended to three days per week in mid-season. Indeed the following season saw the introduction of an additional Sunday cruise to Tarbert, Loch Fyne. Calls at Kilcreggan, incidentally, ceased for all CalMac vessels three years later.

New Ship for Arran
The main development of 1993 was the introduction of the *Caledonian Isles* on the Ardrossan-Brodick route in late August. Even larger than the *Isle of Mull* on which she was modelled, the new ship was the largest ever Clyde steamer, being at 94.28m (308 feet), even longer than the legendary paddle steamer *Columba*, while at 5221 her gross tonnage was ten times as great. Although she did suffer teething problems and there were concerns that her sheer size could cause problems at Ardrossan in severe weather, the *Caledonian Isles* was a very impressive ship and the Arran travellers were very well catered for. She quite outclassed the *Isle of Arran* which she replaced although the older ship herself had been a substantial improvement on her predecessor less than a decade before. Perhaps the Arran route illustrated more than any other the formidable achievements of the Company over a short period of time. The appearance of the new ship as usual caused other vessels to be

When the *Loch Tarbert* arrived at Lochranza for the seasonal service to Claoniag in Kintyre the queues evaporated; she is seen here at Lochranza on her first day in service *IMcC*

CalMac's Clyde cruising vessel *Keppel* alongside Carrick Castle Pier in Loch Goil

CalMac Clyde Cruising was taken up by one of the 'streakers' in 1993 and lasted until 2000; the *Juno* is seen here at Tarbert

The *Saturn* is seen here off Greenock during the visit of the Tall Ships in August 1999   *IMcC*

redeployed. The *Isle of Arran* moved to Kennacraig and became the Islay ferry in summer. The *Claymore* became spare in summer but returned to her previous employment when the *Isle of Arran* became the Company's winter relief vessel.

Further Review

Despite all such attainments the Secretary of State had announced the very day after the launch of the *Caledonian Isles* that the Government intended "to review the possible scope for introducing private sector participation in the provision of Caledonian MacBrayne services." The opposition was swift and virtually unanimous, emphasis being placed on the interchangeability of vessels for relief purposes and in emergency and on cross-subsidisation. Mr Lang later announced that the consultants KPMG had been appointed to review CalMac's whole operation. The Government's case was further weakened when in an official report published in December a different firm of consultants reckoned that a 10% increase on fares, thought to be inevitable on privatisation, would lead to some 700 job losses and would increase migration from the islands to the mainland by 600 over five years. People from all walks of life and from official bodies representing both management and unions remained implacably opposed to any form of privatisation and fragmentation and it was a great relief when KPMG said that such action would make "little economic sense". This was leaked in June 1994 but it was October before the Secretary of State in a written Parliamentary answer confirmed that "the present arrangements for Caledonian MacBrayne represent the most cost-effective and satisfactory way of providing transport for lifeline services off the west coast of Scotland".

That year, 1994, was one of consolidation and modest expansion. New linkspans at Mallaig and Armadale speeded up the turnround periods for the *Iona* and let her revive the overnight sailings from Mallaig to Lochboisdale and Barra. This in turn allowed the *Lord of the Isles* to make one fewer crossing from Oban and so she was able to give an extra weekly sailing, on Tuesday afternoons, to Coll and Tiree. The long-promised crossing between Tarbert and Portavadie became reality in July when the *Rhum* was transferred there. She was supported by Argyll and the Isles Enterprise; this organisation had also paid for the construction of the necessary terminals. It became obvious very quickly that the new service had great potential but progress was limited as a small bow-loader was quite restrictive and all-year-round commercial traffic would not be enticed into using it while it remained seasonal. The *Pioneer*, without regular summer employment for six years, was reintroduced to service as a second full-time Rothesay ferry even expanding her horizons by inaugurating a twice-weekly vehicle service between Rothesay and Brodick. The *Claymore* was now spare vessel but at weekends she reintroduced a service from Ardrossan to Douglas, Isle of Man. For this voyage, operated in association with the Isle of Man Steam Packet Co, she required an International Passenger Certificate. It was the first time CalMac had ever actually rostered one of its fleet to sail furth of Scotland: the *Pioneer* had sailed from Gourock to Douglas in emergency the previous summer but she had been under charter. The *Pioneer's* Brodick leg lasted five years and the *Claymore's* sortie to the Isle of Man only three.

The main development of 1993 was the introduction of the *Caledonian Isles* on the Ardrossan-Brodick route; she was modelled on the *Isle of Mull* and the two ships are seen together at Brodick in February 1997   *Hamish Stewart*

Looking down from the upper deck of the *Claymore* on the motor cyclists about to disembark for the TT Races at Douglas, Isle of Man   *Caledonian MacBrayne*

CalMac had always made the safety of their passengers and crews their number one priority but following the tragic sinking of the *Estonia* in the Baltic with horrendous loss of life safety regulations were tightened both in Britain and across the European Union. New rules were drawn up, known as SOLAS (Safety of Lives at Sea) regulations and they were ever more closely to govern how ships were constructed and what features they possessed. The Company's annual subsidy had to be increased quite considerably so that any new tonnage could incorporate the required features and, where necessary, existing ships modified.

A New Ship for Stornoway
CalMac's strategic plan included the replacement of the ageing *Suilven* for the Stornoway station with a purpose-built vessel. The *Suilven*'s accommodation by now looked distinctly dated, so far had the Company progressed in the intervening years, her vehicle and occasionally her passenger complement was inadequate and she was taking over three and a half hours on passage to Ullapool. Announced in May 1993, ordered the following September from Ferguson's of Port Glasgow and launched by HRH Princess Alexandra in April 1995, the *Isle of Lewis* took over at the end of July of that year. On trials she had reached 18.9 knots, the fastest ever motor vessel in the fleet and arguably surpassed only by the turbine *Saint Columba*. She was 22 feet longer than the *Caledonian Isles* and at 6563 her gross tonnage was appreciably higher. Able to carry nearly a thousand passengers and with a car capacity of 123, including 30 on her hoistable mezzanine decks, she solved all the problems which had built up at a stroke and, as was customary when a new ship appeared on a particular crossing, traffic actually increased in absolute terms. The *Suilven* was sold to New Zealand owners.

Bridge at Last
The other significant event of 1995 was the opening of the toll bridge to Skye in October. There was a carnival atmosphere as the *Loch Dunvegan* and *Loch Fyne* gave their last sailings, dressed overall and with pipers playing "Over the sea to Skye"; there was sadness too for the ending of a way of life tinged with apprehension about the employment prospects of the redundant employees and the political manœuvrings about the bridge tolls. Despite the policy outlined when the sisters were built, there was now agreement between Governement and Company that they should be sold. They remained for many months in dock in Greenock with occasional prospects of a buyer but events were to take an unexpected turn. Meanwhile the dream of a coherent link, if not always by bridge or causeway, among all the inhabited islands of the Outer Hebrides became more of a reality when in March a new "Loch" class vessel was ordered from McTay's of Merseyside to join North Uist directly with Harris rather than via the Uig triangle. At the same time the *Bruernish* underwent trials prospecting for possible sites for a service across the Sound of Barra in the south.

Novel Routes
The new Sound of Harris ferry *Loch Bhrusda* was launched in March 1996. Because the Sound is very shallow in places the Company decided not to use either Voith

CalMac had always made the safety of their passengers and crews their number one priority; the crew of the *Clansman* is seen in the ship's fast rescue craft during a drill in January 2000

J Roderick McCrorie

CalMac's strategic plan included replacement of the ageing Suilven with a purpose-built vessel; the *Isle of Lewis* took up the Stornoway-Ullapool service in July 1995; she is captured here weathering a storm while on an exercise off the Butt of Lewis

John Horne

Schneider or conventional propulsion but the Schottel Pump Jet system so that nothing would protrude under the keel of the vessel. In the event handling her required a great deal of skill. She came north from the Mersey in early May but it was a further month before she was ready for service. Navigation in the Sound was uniquely treacherous even for the West of Scotland and buoys had to be laid to ensure her safe passage. Her début, though late, was spectacularly successful and traffic figures were so encouraging that at the height of the season pre-booking was all but essential. The *Hebridean Isles* now made all her voyages to and from Uig and, with a greater number of crossings between Skye and the Outer Isles, there was a rise in her traffic figures also. In addition, 'double-legging' was no longer required.

For some time the idea of a North Channel service between Campbeltown in Kintyre and Ballycastle in Northern Ireland had been mooted; by 1996 plans were well advanced and the Government's go-ahead was awaited. CalMac, with the *Claymore* available and suitable, made it clear they were interested in carrying out the service and also in providing a connecting link to Rathlin Island with one of their spare Island Class ferries. In the event, with a subsidy from the Northern Ireland Office, the *Bruernish* did go to Ballycastle under charter in December. No subsidy was available for the Campbeltown-Ballycastle link, however. The Secretary of State took the view that under the terms of the undertaking which he had with the Company the route would have to be profitable and he had no indication that this would be so. After a great deal of prevaricating and leaking, he announced in October that the private sector company Sea Containers, through a subsidiary the Argyll & Antrim Steam Packet Co, had agreed to operate the service without a subsidy in summer from June 1997 for three years using the *Claymore*. The CalMac Board members were unwilling to sell their vessel but the Secretary of State directed them to do so. The *Claymore* eventually left the fleet in May 1997 but was chartered back for the winter of 1997/98 to work the Islay run as usual and for the 1998/99 winter as stand-by at Campbeltown. The Campbeltown-Ballycastle crossing lasted only for the three seasons specified in the original agreement. The Rathlin Island service, on the other hand, went from strength to strength, the *Canna* replacing the *Bruernish* as the dedicated ferry and CalMac working the route officially in their own name from April 1997. The *Bruernish* took over the Tarbert-Portavadie route and the *Rhum* was displaced to Scalpay, but her term there was short as a bridge was opened from Kyles Scalpay in December.

The service across the Sound of Mull from Lochaline to Fishnish had been operated since 1986 by the *Isle of Cumbrae*. Apart from being almost twenty years old - for depreciation purposes this was the estimated life of a ship - she lacked good covered accommodation for passengers and the size of her car deck was limiting any real growth in vehicular, especially HGV, traffic. A replacement was ordered from Buckie Shipyard and the *Loch Alainn*, after entering service briefly on the Clyde, took over in July 1997. Her increased capacity (24 cars and 150 passengers) was greatly appreciated but her deeper draught caused problems at Fishnish at low tide. Alterations were made to the slipway but in mid-August the difficulties became academic when she had to be withdrawn from service following a serious

The *Lochmor* on one of her cruises in 1994 sails under the Skye Bridge which is in process of being built
J Aikman Smith

The new Sound of Harris ferry *Loch Bhrusda* manœuvring alongside Leverburgh in July 1996   *IMcC*

The *Canna* became dedicated ferry on the service between Rathlin Island and Ballycastle and from April 1997 worked the route in the name of CalMac rather than under charter   *Hamish M Stewart*

The *Rhum* was displaced to Scalpay in 1997 but her term there was short as a bridge was opened from Kyles Scalpay in December that year; she is seen leaving the slip at Scalpay with the new bridge almost complete in the background   *Hamish M Stewart*

breakdown. The *Isle of Cumbrae*, on the appearance of her newest consort, was transferred to the Colintraive-Rhubodach crossing. This freed the *Loch Riddon*, with the faster ramp, to shift to the Largs-Cumbrae service and the *Loch Striven* to Raasay-Sconser. There was a great deal of timber movement on this particular crossing and the previous ferry *Raasay*, with half the *Loch Striven's* complement of vehicles, could not cope. The *Raasay* came off the station after over twenty years, never having missed a full day's service, and, for the first time, became spare. As far as Lochaline was concerned, all the other suitable ferries to replace the *Loch Alainn* were occupied in their new rôles and the Management had no choice but to reactivate the former Skye ferry *Loch Dunvegan*, still in Greenock's James Watt Dock. The Government had previously given permission for the *Loch Dunvegan* and her sister *Loch Fyne* officially to rejoin the fleet. The *"Dunvegan"* sailed north but within a month she too had suffered a serious breakdown and had to be replaced by the *Loch Fyne*. This time the move was a considerable success and she remained the dedicated Sound of Mull ferry: her large capacity was a great boon to islanders, hauliers and tourists alike.

A New Ship for Oban

The other major plank of CalMac's planning in the mid-nineties was a replacement vessel for the *Lord of the Isles* on the long Oban-Tiree and Oban-Barra'boisdale sailings, not because of speed, which for practical reasons could not be increased, but simply because of capacity. Another factor was that the *Iona*, the last single compartment vessel in the fleet, would not be able to conform to SOLAS 95 regulations and would have to be withdrawn after the 1997 season. The *Claymore* was due to take up the *Iona's* Mallaig-Armadale sailings for 1998 before being replaced by the *Lord of the Isles*, displaced by the new build, the following year. The *Iona* was indeed withdrawn and sold to an Orkney owner but the *Claymore* was unable to take over as planned as she had already been forcibly sold to Sea Containers. Her replacement, then, was required a year earlier than anticipated. This new ship was to carry 90 cars and would be the maximum size of vessel which could operate safely and efficiently on the particular route. Because of tighter safety regulations there would be no cabins under the car deck and only reclining seats would be provided. The keenest tender was submitted by Appledore Shipbuilders of North Devon and so they won the contract in October 1996.

The *Clansman* was named by HRH the Princess Royal in March 1998 and entered service in July. Although this was actually nine months earlier than in the original strategic plan, CalMac was still 'one vessel down' in the early season and the *Lord of the Isles* had to continue on her old route. The *Pioneer* was consequently sent to Mallaig and the Upper Clyde fleet had to operate with three vessels instead of four. CalMac's difficulties were exacerbated, however, when a serious breakdown of the *Isle of Lewis* meant that the *Isle of Mull* had to move to Stornoway to cover her sailings. Fortunately the *Iona* had been surveyed by her new owner - and renamed *Pentalina B* - and so for two or three weeks in April/May she was able to rejoin the CalMac fleet under charter to sail between Oban and Craignure. Once in service, the *Clansman* did settle in very quickly to her dual rôle and, as expected, new traffic was generated. The *Lord of the Isles* duly sailed for Mallaig to become Skye ferry

The new *Clansman* was named by HRH the Princess Royal in March 1998 and entered service on the Isles route from Oban in July; she is seen here at speed on her first day of commercial sailings

Caledonian MacBrayne

The *Clansman* was too long to berth at Tobermory and so calls ceased at the pier; the Lord of the Isles is seen leaving for the last time in April 1998 *J Roderick McCrorie*

but she did not entirely forsake the Outer Isles: she still gave the twice weekly overnight sailings to Lochboisdale or Castlebay. It has to be said that she was altogether too grand a vessel for the sheltered waters crossing and with the *Clansman* conveying increased numbers to the Outer Isles her traffic on that part of the route was rather light. One consequence of the commissioning of the *Clansman*, incidentally, was the cessation of calls at Tobermory Pier, an important link since 1851, as the new ship was too long to berth there. Tobermory had been part of the Inner Isles roster since the days of the *Clydesdale* in 1889; the pier had been closed for renovation and extension in the early 1980s but at that time a tender had been used to serve the ferry as she lay off.

The Small Vessels Jigsaw
As regards the "Loch" and Island Class ferries, the *Loch Alainn* eventually returned to service - but not in the Western Isles. Instead she became the dedicated ferry on the Largs-Cumbrae crossing and a great blessing she turned out to be. Sunday evening queuing when the weekenders tried to leave the island was a thing of the past. Partnering her was still the *Loch Riddon* but the *Loch Linnhe* was able to move to Tarbert for the Portavadie service, at last allowing real drive-through operation there, with immediate positive results. By now this was, as had been hoped, an all-year-round service, and in winter the ferry also made regular trips to Lochranza to convey dangerous cargoes which would otherwise have meant additional sailings for the *Caledonian Isles*. The *Loch Linnhe's* move let the *Bruernish* shift north to Oban to serve Lismore and the *Coll* (which as the Kilchoan ferry had previously switched with the *Eigg*) could be withdrawn. On the sale list with her was the *Rhum*, also no longer required, and the pair made for Donegal to join their two sisters which were already in service there.

In December 1998 a causeway was completed between North Uist and the small island of Berneray. One of the conditions which had been put in place to allow finance for the infrastructure for the Sound of Harris ferry between Otternish and Leverburgh was that CalMac had to take over responsibility for the service to Berneray, previously undertaken by Comhairle nan Eilean Siar, the Western Isles Council. In winter the *Loch Bhrusda* coped on her own but in summer CalMac operated on the Council's behalf the bow-loading ferry *Eilean Bhearnaraigh* to fulfil their obligation for a service between Berneray and Otternish, the nearest point in North Uist. With the opening of the causeway this arrangement ceased and the *Loch Bhrusda* concentrated solely on the Harris run. The Sound of Barra ferry for which CalMac and the Comhairle had been planning was later aborted, at least in the short term, when the Scottish Executive were unable to find the appropriate funding. With devolution in 1999, Scottish Executive Ministers had become the shareholders for Caledonian MacBrayne in lieu of the Secretary of State and the Company had become answerable to them.

The final piece of the 'small vessels' jigsaw was that major alterations were carried out at Colintraive involving the construction of a dolphin at the slipway to allow the ferry to berth alongside overnight. At the very end of March 1999, with the works complete, the *Loch Dunvegan* could take her place as the dedicated Colintraive-

The dedicated Cumbrae ferry *Loch Alainn* at Cumbrae Slip in January 2000. The *Clansman* is seen in the background carrying out a charter for the Clyde River Steamer Club *Hamish M Stewart*

The last piece of the CalMac's small vessels jigsaw came into place in March 1999 when the ex-Skye ferry *Loch Dunvegan* took over as dedicated Colintraive-Rhubodach ferry; she is seen here at Rhubodach in August that year *IMcC*

The Kilchoan ferry was upgraded when the *Loch Linnhe* arrived from the Clyde; she is seen here at Kilchoan, in Ardnamurchan, in August 1999 *Hamish M Stewart*

In 1999 the *Eigg* returned to Lismore but she was rebuilt with a vertical extension to her wheel house so that the chargehand could see forward if she was carrying a high load; the 'tall ship' *Eigg* is seen approaching her berth at Oban *Hamish M Stewart*

Rhubodach ferry, this being the only route on which she could sensibly serve. This let the *Isle of Cumbrae* transfer to Tarbert-Portavadie and the *Loch Linnhe* to make for Tobermory. The Kilchoan ferry, the slipways having been duly broadened, was thus upgraded from a six-car to a twelve-car vessel. The *Eigg* returned to Lismore, but she was rebuilt with a vertical extension to her wheel house so that the chargehand could see forward if she was carrying a high load - a further safety regulation. The *Raasay* remained spare and relief at Oban, giving periodic cargo and livestock runs to the Small Isles, and the *Bruernish* fulfilled a similar rôle on the Clyde.

Ships for a New Millennium
In July 1998 the Secretary of State announced that CalMac was to receive £20 million to build two ferries, one for the Small Isles to replace the *Lochmor* which would be withdrawn and one for the Uig station to replace the *Hebridean Isles* which would be cascaded for further service. As with the *Lochmor* herself, extensive consultation was used to find the optimum design and the optimum *modus operandi*. With help from the EC, all the Small Isles would eventually be given appropriate slipways, as would Inverie in Loch Nevis. The ship, designed for 12 cars and 200 passengers, was to be sufficiently adaptable to use these slipways and the linkspan at Mallaig. In the interim period she would have to load and unload in the time-honoured way - by flitboat. Ailsa of Troon won the order. During construction her design was altered as it had become obvious that some of the slipways would not be ready for a considerable time after her commissioning. The ship was duly launched as *Lochnevis* in May 2000 by Ms Sarah Boyack, MSP, the Minister for Transport and the Environment. For unconnected reasons, the Troon yard was very soon closed and this, together with the sophistication and uniqueness of the vessel, delayed her fitting out. She ran trials in September, was handed over a month later and was ready to enter service in November. The *Lochnevis* presented a very marked contrast to her predecessor, only twenty years her senior and, incidentally, the last ship to be ordered by CalMac from Ailsa. The electronic wizardry apparent in her navigating bridge and engine room, the roomy and superior accommodation for a vessel of her size and the huge stern ramp needed for her unique rôle made her a remarkable little vessel. She was also relatively fast and the timetable had to be recast for her. On her appearance the *Lochmor* moved to Tobermory Bay and placed on the sale list. The flitboat at Eigg, the *Ulva*, last of MacBrayne's red boats, was worn out and was replaced in December 2000 by a new build from Corpach, the *Laig Bay*.

It was in August 2000 that HM the Queen launched from Ferguson's, Port Glasgow, the last major ship to be built in the Company's first 150 years. The *Hebrides* was destined for Uig and her design, after considerable consultation, was virtually a repeat of the *Clansman*, with a few minor improvements. She ran trials in January 2001 and was due to enter service in March. When she did capacity on the Lochmaddy and Tarbert routes would be increased by 50%. The bell of the first *Hebrides*, of 1898, was due to be presented to her as a symbol of her heritage. The *Hebridean Isles* would then move to Islay and the *Isle of Arran* would become spare, an essential feature the Company had not had in summer since the enforced sale of the *Claymore*.

The new Small Isles ferry was launched as *Lochnevis* in May 2000 by Sarah Boyack, MSP

Hamish M Stewart

Both the Small Isles ferry *Lochmor* and the flitboat *Ulva* were placed on the sale list in late 2000; they are seen here at Eigg in July 1999

S Forrest

A Problem Solved?

Apart from the introduction of new tonnage, there were other matters occupying the CalMac Board at the start of the new millennium. Since 1983 the Company had been operating their Gourock-Dunoon service at the frequency of one sailing per hour, with a modest enhancement in the morning and early evening. As a result partly of this limitation on CalMac's operation, Western Ferries were able to forge ahead and by the late 1990's had acquired some 80% of the vehicle traffic and 60% of the passenger traffic (largely car-based) on the route. In the long term the Government reckoned that the arrangement whereby two operators competed was neither sustainable nor suitable because of the high cost to the taxpayer. The state-owned operator would have to receive both a subsidy and a grant for investment in replacement vessels although it was in competition with the private sector. The result was that in 1997, just days before the General Election, the Conservative Government commissioned a firm of accountants, Deloitte & Touche, to examine future prospects for the services between Inverclyde and Cowal and come up with a range of options. The report was ready six months later but it was not 'leaked' for a further twelve months.

The consultants had concluded that the *status quo* was not a cheap option for the public purse. The CalMac route required medium-term investment both in vessels and in pier infrastructure; the 'streakers' were 25 years old and the century-old Dunoon Pier itself, with its side-loading linkspan and vulnerability to weather, was in a fairly parlous state. Such investment could not be made using commercial finance but only with substantial public sector support. The consultants reckoned that either company could continue satisfactorily on its own, except at the annual Cowal Games weekend, when chartering would be needed. A single service à la Western Ferries, although perhaps commercially viable, would mean that consumer choice and competition would be lost and would mark an end to direct ferry travel to Dunoon Pier, in the town centre. Deloitte & Touche also reported on the CalMac initiative to invest in two new ro-ro double-ended vessels and run them from a concrete slipway near the old Pier at Dunoon, crewing being distinctly cheaper. Alternatively, they argued, Western Ferries could continue carrying cars and CalMac could operate a complementary centre-to-centre service for foot passengers only. When eventually the report was published, the Scottish Executive, having taken over responsibility from Westminster, made no definite response, until early in 2001 when they recommended subsidising only a passenger service between Gourock and Dunoon.

New Horizons

In the late summer of 1998 the Government advertised for "expressions of interest" from companies who might consider providing services to the Northern Isles of Orkney and Shetland from April 2002. The operators on the route, P&O Scottish Ferries, owned four second hand vessels which gave one direct crossing between Aberdeen and Lerwick in Shetland and one between Scrabster and Stromness in Orkney, together with an indirect sailing and a cargo vessel service from Aberdeen to both islands. CalMac were to be allowed to tender "on the basis that providing vessels for the route would not add to the public expenditure requirements". The

The *Hebrides*, launched in August 2000 from Ferguson's, Port Glasgow, was the last ship to be built in the Company's first 150 years; she was destined for Uig   *Iain McPherson*

The *Saturn* having just unloaded her Dunoon traffic at Gourock and the *Pioneer* at the lay up berth or 'wires' in 1998   *J Roderick McCrorie*

franchise to operate the service was to be for a period of five years as determined by the EC requirements for the periodic tendering of State Aids subsidies. The CalMac Board sought partners who would have the finance to build and then lease three new vessels to take over the three main routes, the intention being to charter a suitable cargo vessel. First Wightlink, followed by National Express, and then, when these agreements fell through, the Royal Bank of Scotland undertook to fulfil that rôle.

The Company consulted widely as to the wishes of the islanders and others involved in the service. According to island sources the whole bidding process under the ægis of the Scottish Executive took an interminable time and there certainly was a deal of slippage. The starting date for the implementation of the new franchise, however, was also put back, from April till October 2002. In late June 2000 CalMac, under the working project name Northlink Orkney & Shetland Services, made public details of their bid. Two large vessels of 125m and 12,000 tons would carry 600 passengers at 24 knots and at lower fares between Aberdeen and Shetland, one sailing via Orkney. Meanwhile a third smaller ship of 110m and 8 600 tons would sail between Stromness and Scrabster in a mere 90 minutes, again with a passenger complement of 600. All cabins were to be en suite and there was to be a choice of restaurants, bars and lounges, a children's play area and, on the larger vessels, a cinema.

At last on 6 October 2000 the Transport Minister announced the result of the tendering process - and Northlink was the preferred bidder. A great deal of further work was necessary before the contract was signed but the Minister finally gave her approval just before Christmas. The smaller Pentland Firth ferry was to have been built by Ferguson's, Port Glasgow, but they had to pull out because of design capacity difficulties and the short timescale. Aker Finnyards of Rauma in Finland, the yard which was to build the other two vessels, agreed to complete the third also, and were confident they could do so in time.

State Aids
At the start of the new millennium public concern was being expressed that the European Commission was investigating the level of CalMac's subsidy to check that it complied with the rules on state aid or if it distorted the market. It was in late April that Sarah Boyack, MSP, announced that to comply with Articles 87 and 88 of the Treaty of Amsterdam CalMac's subsidy had to be justified by having routes put out to competitive tender, as in the Northern Isles. Put another way, each subsidised route carried a Public Service Obligation (PSO) which meant that it had to satisfy fixed standards of continuity, regularity, capacity and pricing which would not necessarily pertain if economic factors alone were taken into account: each PSO had to be investigated. Tenders were to be invited later in 2000 for confirmation of contracts in 2001. At the same time the Minister launched a consultation exercise "Delivering Lifeline Ferry Services" to run until 30 June.

Both the *Isle of Lewis* and the *Clansman* 'showed the flag' at Stromness, Orkney, during the bidding process for the Northern Isles franchise; the Isle of Lewis is seen here at the terminal in November 1998
Alastair Cormack

A computer image of the new Orkney and Shetland ferries as envisaged by Northlink

A summary of the responses to the exercise was made public in January 2001. There had been 110 responses and the general tone had been fairly constructive, although concern was expressed over any proposed change, with suspicions - unfounded - that the Scottish Executive were pursuing a privatisation agenda. There had been quite strong support for a vessel-owning company, perhaps because the contract for operating each route was to run only for five years and there would therefore be problems if operators themselves had to fund vessels. Respondents overwhelmingly expressed a preference for the network to be tendered as a whole, to prevent predators cherry-picking lucrative routes. There was strong support too for the continuation of subsidy to mainland-to-mainland services, especially where they served remote peninsulas (including local authority links). Several responses mentioned the importance of continued cooperation between operators, through-ticketing and holistic marketing and the preparation of a timetable covering the whole network.

In a detailed statement made at the same time Ms Boyack gave notice of her presentation to the EC, in which she incorporated many of the points brought out in the consulation exercise. She said that she regarded all CalMac island ferry services as being consistent with PSOs and she planned to tender these services in line with regulations. She had already made robust representations about the Company's mainland-to-mainland services and had received a favourable response. She indicated that it was the Executive's strong preference that the network be tendered as a whole to maximise reliablity, simplify ship management, provide economies of scale, avoid cherry-picking and facilitate an integrated transport system. She proposed a public sector owning company where the existing CalMac vessels, together with piers and harbours, would be leased to operators on a bare boat basis, although much-needed replacement tonnage would be allowed in the five year period. She made it clear that CalMac would be allowed to bid to operate the routes on a basis "which ensured that the bid was prepared on a fair and full cost basis and evaluated transparently and equally with bids from other potential operators".

As the Company's 150th Anniversary approached the Board was setting out details of its plans on how best to proceed so that the name 'MacBrayne' would continue to be synonymous with the delivering of lifeline services to the islands off the west coast of Scotland.

150 Years
As in 1951, the ships of the fleet were dressed overall on the occasion of the Company's 150th Anniversary, 10 Feburary 2001. The Hutcheson Memorial on Kerrera was also illuminated.

During the summer following, the distribution of vessels over the Company's various routes is shown below. Because of the extent of the changes, any direct comparison with 1951 is meaningless. All the ships are motor vessels and so the M.V. is omitted.

Gourock-Dunoon	*Juno*
Rothesay-Wemyss Bay	*Jupiter*
	Saturn
	Pioneer
Ardrossan-Brodick	*Caledonian Isles*
Largs-Cumbrae Slip	*Loch Alainn*
	Loch Riddon
Colintraive-Rhubodach	*Loch Dunvegan*
Tarbert-Portavadie	*Isle of Cumbrae*
Lochranza-Claonaig	*Loch Tarbert*
Kennacraig-Islay (-Colonsay)	*Hebridean Isles*
Oban-Mull (-Colonsay)	*Isle of Mull*
Oban-Coll-Tiree/Barra'boisdale/	*Clansman*
Colonsay	
Mallaig-Armadale/Outer Isles	*Lord of the Isles*
Mallaig-Small Isles	*Lochnevis*
Tarbert/Lochmaddy-Uig	*Hebrides*
Stornoway-Ullapool	*Isle of Lewis*
Gigha-Tayinloan	*Loch Ranza*
Oban-Lismore	*Eigg*
Lochaline-Fishnish	*Loch Fyne*
Tobermory-Kilchoan	*Loch Linnhe*
Fionnphort-Iona	*Loch Buie*
Raasay-Sconser	*Loch Striven*
Berneray-Leverburgh	*Loch Bhrusda*
Rathlin Island-Ballycastle	*Canna*
Eigg flitboat	*Laig Bay*
Spare (major units)	*Isle of Arran*
Spare (minor ferries)	*Bruernish*
	Raasay

From modest beginnings using eight small iron or wooden paddle steamers the Company had expanded and now had vessels from 70 to almost 7000 tons capable in some cases of transporting hundreds of passengers, scores of cars and several heavy vehicles on a single journey. No longer did a steamship wend its leisurely way from the centre of Glasgow and reach its destination three days later: instead a motor vessel sailed, by and large, on the shortest crossing from mainland to island, usually several times in one day. For a large part of the era of the motor car, vehicles were slowly loaded by derrick into the ship's cargo hold: for a few years they were loaded on hydraulic lifts while in the new millennium they drove on and drove off, the car deck being unloaded and loaded again in a few minutes. In the beginning only monied travellers would be found aboard, except during Glasgow Fair when cheap fares enticed the 'humbler classes' to go for an excursion in their droves: now, in a more egalitarian culture, the ships were single-class and catered for everyone. As a result, some of the grace and elegance of the old paddle steamers, like the silver service in the dining room, the gold lines on the hull and the gleaming brass of the steampipes, had gone: the modern ships were mini-liners with cafeterias, children's play areas, invalid lifts and dog kennels. Travellers have been enticed aboard through the ages by the lure of the "Royal Route", the prestige of the "Royal Mail Steamer", the image of the MacBrayne Highlander in the Company's literature and the adroit use of the "Marine Motorway" and "Hebridean Driveaway". They have been exhorted to take part in circular tours, rail tours, coach tours, mini tours and to buy Hopscotch tickets, Early Bird Savers and Car Rovers. The Company has never been more committed to passenger safety and comfort and runs a standard of service which could not have been envisaged by previous generations. Steamers may have become ferries and piers ferry terminals but the officers and crews which are the heart of the ships have not changed and the lure of the islands of the west remains undiminished over the years.

The old: a view of the engines of the *Glengarry* (1844)

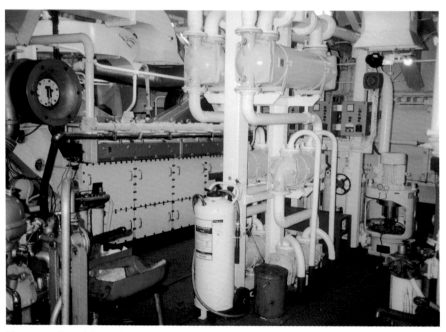

The new: a view of the engines of the *Claymore* (1978)

Lawrence J Macduff

The old: the dining saloon of the *Iona* (1864)

The new: the cafeteria of the *Isle of Mull* (1988)

The old: the three majestic funnels of the *Saint Columba* (1912)

The new: the futuristic funnel of the *Isle of Mull* (1988)

The old: the famous Captain 'Squeaky' Robertson on the bridge of the *Lochmor*

The new: CalMac's first female master, Captain Linda Ward on the *Juno*　　*IMcC*

Five CalMac vessels in Oban Bay make for a very busy photograph; the *Raasay* is nearest the camera with the *Eigg* alongside, the *Isle of Mull* is at the linkspan with the *Clansman* beyond at the Railway Pier while the *Lord of the Isles* is berthed at the North Pier
Hamish M Stewart

173

Fleet List of
David Hutcheson & Company (1851-79)
David MacBrayne (1879-1905)
David MacBrayne Ltd (1906-28)
David MacBrayne (1928) Ltd (1928-34)
David MacBrayne Ltd (1934-72)
Caledonian MacBrayne Ltd (1973-2001)*
* and subsidiaries

This is a simplified list of the major Hutcheson/MacBrayne/Caledonian MacBrayne vessels from 1851 until 2001. Gross tonnage refers to the original figure in the Company's ownership for the particular ship, date of completion means the year in which the ship was ready to enter service and date of withdrawal when the vessel stopped sailing for the Company (as distinct from the date of sale).

Ship	Type	Tonnage	Completed	Acquired	Withdrawn
Curlew	P.S.	92	1837	1851	1853
Shandon	P.S.	186	1839	1851	1852
Duntroon Castle	P.S.	176	1842	1851	1853
Dolphin	P.S.	121	1844	1851	1862
Edinburgh Castle/					
Glengarry (1875)	P.S.	114	1844	1851	1927
Pioneer	P.S.	196	1844	1851	1893
Cygnet	P.S.	101	1848	1851	1882
Lapwing	P.S.	101	1848	1851	1859
Mountaineer	P.S.	173	1852	1852	1889
Chevalier	P.S.	229	1853	1853	1854
Iona	P.S.	325	1855	1855	1862
Clansman	P.S.	414	1855	1855	1869
Inverary Castle/					
Inveraray Castle (1874)	P.S.	120	1839	1857	1891
Mary Jane/Glencoe (1875)	P.S.	211	1846	1857	1931
Duke of Argyll	P.S.	101	1852	1857	1858
Stork	P.S.	396	1851	1858	1861
Plover ex *Maid of Lorn*	P.S.	120	1849	1859	1879
Fingal	S.S.	352	1860	1861	1861
Fairy	P.S.	151	1861	1861	1863
Clydesdale	S.S.	403	1862	1862	1905
Iona	P.S.	368	1863	1863	1863
Staffa	S.S.	268	1863	1863	1886
Iona	P.S.	393	1864	1864	1935
Gondolier	P.S.	173	1866	1866	1939
Chevalier	P.S.	292	1866	1866	1927

Linnet	S.S.	33	1866	1866	1928
Dolphin ex *Islay*	P.S.	325	1849	1868	1868
Clansman	S.S.	600	1870	1870	1909
Queen of the Lake	S.S.	51	1863	1876	1882
Lochawe	S.S.	97	1876	1876	1914
Islay	P.S.	362	1867	1876	1890
Lochiel	S.S.	262	1877	1877	1907
Fingal	S.S.	124	1878	1878	1917
Columba	P.S.	543	1878	1878	1935
Claymore	S.S.	726	1881	1882	1931
Cavalier	S.S.	369	1883	1883	1919
Grenadier	P.S.	372	1885	1885	1927
Lochness ex *Lough Foyle* ex *Loch Goil*	P.S.	121	1853	1885	1912
Ethel/Clansman (1910)	S.S.	281	1880	1885	1916
Handa ex *Aros Castle*	S.S.	146	1876	1887	1917
Mabel	S.S.	28	1883	1887	1911
Countess of Kellie	S.S.	95	1870	1887	1904
Udea	S.S.	157	1873	1888	1894
Staffa ex *Adela*	S.S.	211	1861	1888	1919
Fusilier	P.S.	251	1888	1888	1934
Texa ex *James Mutter*	S.S.	157	1884	1889	1914
Flowerdale ex *Recovery*	S.S.	488	1878	1889	1904
Hero/Mountaineer (1892)	P.S.	178	1858	1890	1909
Islay ex *Princess Louise*	P.S.	497	1872	1890	1902
Great Western Lovedale (1893)	P.S.	459	1867	1891	1904
Gael	P.S.	419	1867	1891	1923
Cygnus/Brigadier (1893)	P.S.	250	1854	1891	1896
Carabinier ex *Albert Edward*	P.S.	299	1878	1893	1908
Gairlochy ex *Ardmore* ex *Sultan*	P.S.	142	1861	1894	1919
Glendale ex *La Belgique*, etc	P.S.	511	1875	1902	1905
Lapwing	S.S.	211	1903	1903	1917
Sheila	S.S.	280	1904	1904	1927
Plover/Loch Aline (1934)	S.S.	208	1904	1904	1939
Cygnet	S.S.	115	1904	1904	1930
Brenda	S.S.	115	1905	1905	1929
Pioneer	P.S.	241	1905	1905	1943
Clydesdale	S.S.	394	1905	1905	1953
Comet ex *Win*	M.V.	43	1905	1907	1946
Scout	M.V.	82	1907	1907	1913
Chieftain	S.S.	1081	1907	1907	1919
Lochinvar	M.V.	178	1908	1908	1960
Lochiel	S.S.	241	1908	1908	1917

Nellie/Staffa (1910)	S.S.	89	1892	1980	1916
Dirk	S.S.	181	1909	1909	1917
Mountaineer	P.S.	235	1910	1910	1937
Cona	M.V.		1906	1911	1917
Loch Leven Queen/					
Lochness (1912)	S.S.	82	1896	1911	1928
Countess of Mayo	S.S.	46	1897	1914	1917
Devonia/Lochiel (1920)	S.S.	326	1906	1919	1938
Lochdunvegan					
ex *Denbigh Coast* etc	S.S.	411	1891	1929	1948
Lochness	S.S.	777	1929	1929	1955
Lochshiel	M.V.	208	1929	1929	1952
Lochearn	M.V.	542	1930	1930	1964
Lochmor	M.V.	542	1930	1930	1964
Lochbroom ex *City of London*	S.S.	1139	1871	1931	1936
Lochfyne	M.V.	748	1931	1931	1969
Princess Louise	S.S.	106	1898	1934	1938
Lochnevis	M.V.	568	1934	1934	1969
Saint Columba					
ex *Queen Alexandra*	T.S.	792	1912	1935	1958
King George V	T.S.	797	1926	1935	1974
Lochgorm ex *Lairdspool*					
ex *Lily*	S.S.	635	1896	1937	1951
Lochgarry ex *Lairdsrock*					
ex *Vulture*	S.S.	1670	1898	1937	1939
Lochbuie	M.V.	40	1938	1938	1939
Lochiel	M.V.	580	1939	1939	1970
Loch Seaforth	M.V.	1089	1947	1947	1973
Lochnell	M.V.	31	1941	1947	1981
Dunara Castle	S.S.	423	1875	1948	1948
Challenger	S.S.	151	1897	1948	1948
Hebrides	S.S.	585	1898	1948	1955
Lochbroom ex *Empire Maysong*	M.V.	413	1945	1948	1970
Lochbuie	M.V.	37	1942	1949	1968
Loch Frisa ex *Marleen*	S.S.	338	1946	1949	1963
Lochdunvegan ex *Örnen*	M.V.	562	1948	1950	1973
Loch Carron	M.V.	650	1951	1951	1975
Claymore	M.V.	1024	1955	1955	1975
Loch Ard	M.V.	611	1955	1955	1970
Loch Toscaig ex *Irene Julia* etc.	M.V.	49	1945	1955	1975
Loch Arkaig	M.V.	179	1942	1959	1979

Loch Eynort ex *Valonia*	M.V.	117	1947	1961	1970
Hebrides	M.V.	2104	1964	1964	1985
Clansman	M.V.	2104	1964	1964	1984
Columba	M.V.	2104	1964	1964	1988
Scalpay	M.V.	24	1957	1965	1971
Arran	M.V.	568	1953	1969	1979
Iona	M.V.	1192	1970	1970	1997
Scalpay	M.V.	24	1956	1971	1979
Kilbrannan	M.V.	64	1972	1973	1992
Morvern	M.V.	64	1972	1973	1995
Queen Mary II/					
Queen Mary (1976)	T.S.	1014	1933	1973	1977
Waverley	P.S.	693	1947	1973	1973
Maid of the Loch	P.S.	555	1953	1973	1981
Maid of Argyll	M.V.	508	1953	1973	1973
Maid of Cumbrae	M.V.	508	1953	1973	1978
Cowal	M.V.	569	1954	1973	1977
Bute	M.V.	568	1954	1973	1978
Glen Sannox	M.V.	1269	1957	1973	1989
Largs ex *Kyleakin II*					
ex *Kyleakin*	M.V.	60	1960	1973	1983
Portree	M.V.	65	1965	1973	1986
Broadford	M.V.	64	1966	1973	1986
Keppel ex *Rose*	M.V.	214	1961	1973	1992
Coruisk	M.V.	60	1969	1973	1986
Caledonia ex *Stena Baltica*	M.V.	1157	1966	1973	1987
Kyleakin	M.V.	225	1970	1973	1991
Lochalsh	M.V.	225	1971	1973	1991
Bruernish	M.V.	69	1973	1973	
Rhum	M.V.	69	1973	1973	1998
Coll	M.V.	69	1973	1973	1998
Jupiter	M.V.	849	1973	1974	
Pioneer	M.V.	1071	1974	1974	
Suilven	M.V.	1908	1974	1974	1995
Juno	M.V.	854	1974	1974	
Eigg	M.V.	69	1974	1975	
Canna	M.V.	69	1975	1976	
Raasay	M.V.	69	1976	1976	
Isle of Cumbrae	M.V.	201	1976	1977	
Saturn	M.V.	851	1977	1978	
Claymore	M.V.	1580	1978	1979	1997
Lochmor	M.V.	189	1979	1979	2000
Isle of Arran	M.V.	3296	1983	1984	
Hebridean Isles	M.V.	3040	1985	1985	
Loch Striven	M.V.	206	1986	1986	

Loch Linnhe	M.V.	206	1986	1986
Loch Riddon	M.V.	206	1986	1986
Loch Ranza	M.V.	206	1986	1987
Isle of Mull	M.V.	4300	1988	1988
Lord of the Isles	M.V.	3504	1989	1989
Loch Dunvegan	M.V.	550	1991	1991
Loch Fyne	M.V.	550	1991	1991
Loch Buie	M.V.	295	1991	1992
Loch Tarbert	M.V.	211	1992	1992
Caledonian Isles	M.V.	5221	1993	1993
Isle of Lewis	M.V.	6753	1995	1995
Loch Bhrusda	M.V.	246	1996	1996
Loch Alainn	M.V.	396	1997	1997
Clansman	M.V.	5499	1998	1998
Lochnevis	M.V.	941	2000	2000
Hebrides	M.V.	5500	2000	2001

ACKNOWLEDGEMENTS

In writing this book, in addition to making use of my own research, I have called upon the painstaking work carried out over the years by several individuals. Prominent among them are Iain C MacArthur, and the late Graham E Langmuir, Ian Shannon and James Aikman Smith: I freely acknowledge the very considerable contribution they have made to the ever increasing pool of knowledge about Clyde and West Highland steamers. Primary sources have included Harbour and other records of what is now the Clyde Port Authority, various newspapers, primarily "The Oban Times", and minute books of the various companies involved in the story. I am especially grateful to the Chairman and certain Directors of Caledonian MacBrayne and to Derek Crawford and Iain MacArthur for reading the manuscript and using their wide knowledge to correct any errors in the text.

The photographs and reproductions of artefacts are from my own collection. Where possible I have acknowledged the sources and where possible have sought permission for their inclusion. If, through ignorance of the identity of any photographer, I have omitted his or her name in the caption, I apologise. The photographs of the fleet as in summer 2001 at the end of the book were taken by Hamish Stewart. I acknowledge the assistance of Iain Quinn in matters of identification.

I feel privileged at being asked by CalMac to write the story of "Royal Road to the Isles, 150 Years of MacBrayne Shipping" and am very grateful for the unstinting support given by many of the Company's Directors and Managers wherever it was needed during the project's gestation. Caledonian MacBrayne itself, as the text makes clear, was formed in 1973 and, legalistically, was The Caledonian Steam Packet Company of 1889 renamed. The name MacBrayne, however, has been intimately associated with the company since 1851 and before and this makes it totally legitimate to celebrate the 150th Anniversary in 2001. Theirs is a proud history and I am proud to have been instrumental in making it more widely known.

IAN McCRORIE

Caledonian MacBrayne
Hebridean and Clyde Ferries

THE FLEET

JUNO
Gourock-Dunoon,
Wemyss Bay-Rothesay

Built: 1974,
James Lamont & Co. Ltd.,
Port Glasgow;
Gross tons: 853.71;
Length: 66.45m;
Breadth: 13.80m;
Draught: 2.45m;
Speed: 12kts;
Passengers: 531;
Crew: 10;
Cars 40.

JUPITER
Wemyss Bay-Rothesay,
Gourock-Dunoon

Built: 1974,
James Lamont & Co. Ltd.,
Port Glasgow;
Gross tons: 848.61;
Length: 66.45m;
Breadth: 13.80m;
Draught: 2.45m;
Speed: 12kts;
Passengers: 531;
Crew: 10;
Cars 40.

PIONEER
Gourock-Dunoon and
relief vessel

Built: 1974,
Robb Caledon
Shipbuilders Ltd., Leith;
Gross tons: 1071;
Length: 67.00m;
Breadth: 13.40m;
Draught: 2.40m;
Speed: 16kts;
Passengers: 218;
Crew: 15;
Cars 32.

SATURN
**Wemyss Bay-Rothesay,
Gourock-Dunoon**

Built: 1978,
Ailsa Shipbuilding Co. Ltd.,
Troon;
Gross tons: 851.26;
Length: 69.50m;
Breadth: 13.80m;
Draught: 2.45m;
Speed: 12kts;
Passengers: 531;
Crew: 10;
Cars 40.

CALEDONIAN ISLES
Ardrossan-Brodick

Built: 1993,
Richards Shipbuilders,
Lowestoft;
Gross tons: 5221;
Length: 94.00m;
Breadth: 15.80m;
Draught: 3.20m;
Speed: 15kts;
Passengers: 1000;
Crew: 28;
Cars 110.

CLANSMAN
**Oban-Coll-Tiree/
Barra-Lochboisdale/
Colonsay**

Built: 1998,
Appledore Shipbuilders,
Devon;
Gross tons: 5499;
Length: 99.00m;
Breadth: 15.80m;
Draught: 3.22m;
Speed: 16.5kts;
Passengers: 638;
Crew: 28;
Cars 100.

HEBRIDEAN ISLES
Kennacraig-Islay
(-Colonsay-Oban)

Built: 1985,
Cochrane Shipbuilders,
Selby;
Gross tons: 3040;
Length: 85.15m;
Breadth: 15.80m;
Draught: 3.11m;
Speed: 15kts;
Passengers: 494;
Crew: 24;
Cars 68.

HEBRIDES
Tarbert/Lochmaddy-Uig

Built: 2000,
Ferguson Shipbuilders,
Port Glasgow;
Gross tons: 5506;
Length: 99.00m;
Breadth: 15.80m;
Draught: 3.22m;
Speed: 16.5kts;
Passengers: 612;
Crew: 24;
Cars 110.

ISLE OF ARRAN
Relief vessel

Built: 1984,
Ferguson Ailsa Ltd.,
Port Glasgow;
Gross tons: 3296;
Length: 84.90m;
Breadth: 15.80m;
Draught: 3.20m;
Speed: 15kts;
Passengers: 659 max:
Crew: 24;
Cars 68.

ISLE OF MULL
**Oban-Craignure/
Colonsay**

Built: 1988,
Appledore Ferguson Ltd.,
Port Glasgow;
Gross tons: 4719;
Length: 90.03m;
Breadth: 15.80m;
Draught: 3.19m;
Speed: 15kts;
Passengers: 962;
Crew: 28;
Cars 80.

ISLE OF LEWIS
Stornoway-Ullapool

Built: 1995,
Ferguson Shipbuilders Ltd.,
Port Glasgow;
Gross tons: 6753;
Length: 101.25m;
Breadth: 18.52m;
Draught: 4.19m;
Speed: 18kts;
Passengers: 970 max:
Crew: 30;
Cars 123.

LORD OF THE ISLES
**Mallaig-Armadale/
Barra/Lochboisdale**

Built: 1989,
Appledore Ferguson Ltd.,
Port Glasgow;
Gross tons: 3504;
Length: 84.60m;
Breadth: 15.80m;
Draught: 3.19m;
Speed: 16kts;
Passengers: 506;
Crew: 26;
Cars 56.

ISLE OF CUMBRAE
Tarbert-Portavadie

Built: 1977,
Ailsa Shipbuilding Co. Ltd.,
Troon;
Gross tons: 201;
Length: 32.00m;
Breadth: 10.00m;
Draught: 1.40m;
Speed: 8.5kts;
Passengers: 238;
Crew: 4;
Cars 18.

LOCH ALAINN
Largs-Cumbrae Slip

Built: 1998,
Buckie Shipyard,
Buckie;
Gross tons: 396;
Length: 43.54m;
Breadth: 13.40m;
Draught: 3.00m;
Speed: 10kts;
Passengers: 150;
Crew: 4;
Cars 24.

LOCH BHRUSDA
Berneray-Leverburgh

Built: 1996,
McTay Marine,
Liverpool;
Gross tons: 246;
Length: 44.00m;
Breadth: 11.20m;
Draught: 1.50m;
Speed: 10kts;
Passengers: 150;
Crew: 4;
Cars 18.

LOCH BUIE
Fionnphort-Iona

Built: 1992,
J W Miller & Sons Ltd.,
St Monans;
Gross tons: 295;
Length: 30.20m;
Breadth: 10.00m;
Draught: 1.60m;
Speed: 9kts;
Passengers: 250;
Crew: 5;
Cars Nil.

LOCH DUNVEGAN
Colintraive-Rhubodach

Built: 1991,
Ferguson Shipbuilders Ltd.,
Port Glasgow;
Gross tons: 549;
Length: 54.20m;
Breadth: 13.00m;
Draught: 1.60m;
Speed: 8kts;
Passengers: 200;
Crew: 4;
Cars 36.

LOCH FYNE
Lochaline-Fishnish

Built: 1991,
Ferguson Shipbuilders Ltd.,
Port Glasgow;
Gross tons: 549;
Length: 54.20m;
Breadth: 13.00m;
Draught: 1.60m;
Speed: 9kts;
Passengers: 200;
Crew: 4;
Cars 36.

LOCH LINNHE
Tobermory-Kilchoan

Built: 1986,
Richard Dunstan
(Hessle) Ltd.;
Gross tons: 206;
Length: 30.20m;
Breadth: 10.00m;
Draught: 1.50m;
Speed: 9kts;
Passengers: 199;
Crew: 4;
Cars 12.

LOCH RANZA
Gigha-Tayinloan

Built: 1986,
Richard Dunstan
(Hessle) Ltd.;
Gross tons: 206;
Length: 30.20m;
Breadth: 10.00m;
Draught: 1.50m;
Speed: 9kts;
Passengers: 199;
Crew: 4;
Cars 12.

LOCH RIDDON
Largs-Cumbrae Slip

Built: 1986,
Richard Dunstan
(Hessle) Ltd.;
Gross tons: 206;
Length: 30.20m;
Breadth: 10.00m;
Draught: 1.50m;
Speed: 9kts;
Passengers: 199;
Crew: 4;
Cars 12.

LOCH STRIVEN
Raasay-Sconser

Built: 1986,
Richard Dunstan
(Hessle) Ltd.;
Gross tons: 206;
Length: 30.20m;
Breadth: 10.00m;
Draught: 1.50m;
Speed: 9kts;
Passengers: 199;
Crew: 4;
Cars 12.

LOCH TARBERT
Lochranza-Claonaig

Built: 1992,
J W Miller & Sons Ltd.,
St Monans;
Gross tons: 211;
Length: 30.20m;
Breadth: 10.00m;
Draught: 1.60m;
Speed: 9kts;
Passengers: 149;
Crew: 4;
Cars 18.

LOCHNEVIS
Mallaig-Small Isles

Built: 2000,
Ailsa Shipbuilders,
Troon;
Gross tons: 941;
Length: 49.20m;
Breadth: 11.40m;
Draught: 2.65m;
Speed: 13kts;
Passengers: 190;
Crew: 9;
Cars 14.

BRUERNISH
Spare (minor vessels - based Clyde)

Built: 1973,
James Lamont & Co. Ltd.,
Port Glasgow;
Gross tons: 69;
Length: 22.50m;
Breadth: 6.40m;
Draught: 1.40m;
Speed: 8kts;
Passengers: 121 max;
Crew: 4;
Cars 6.

CANNA
**Ballycastle-Rathlin Island
(Northern Ireland)**

Built: 1975,
James Lamont & Co. Ltd.,
Port Glasgow;
Gross tons: 69;
Length: 22.50m;
Breadth: 6.40m;
Draught: 1.40m;
Speed: 8kts;
Passengers: 140 max;
Crew: 4;
Cars 6.

EIGG
Oban-Lismore

Built: 1976,
James Lamont & Co. Ltd.,
Port Glasgow;
Gross tons: 69;
Length: 22.50m;
Breadth: 6.40m;
Draught: 1.40m;
Speed: 8kts;
Passengers: 75 max;
Crew: 3;
Cars 6.

188

RAASAY
Spare (minor vessels - based Oban)

Built: 1975,
James Lamont & Co. Ltd.,
Port Glasgow;
Gross tons: 69;
Length: 22.50m;
Breadth: 6.40m;
Draught: 1.40m;
Speed: 8kts;
Passengers: 75 max;
Crew: 3;
Cars 6.

LAIG BAY
Flitboat at Eigg

Built: 2000,
Corpach Boatbuilding
Company;
Length: 10.50m;
Breadth: 3.80m;
Draught: 1.00m;
Speed: 9kts;
Passengers: 28;
Crew: 2.